the child who walks alone

CASE STUDIES OF REJECTION IN THE SCHOOLS

Library of Congress Cataloging in Publication Data

Stilwell, Anne, 1916—
  The child who walks alone.

  1. Problem children—Education—Texas.   I. Stilwell,
Hart, 1902-   joint author.   II. Title.
LC4692.T4S8   371.9'3   79-38569
ISBN 978-0-292-74187-4

www.utpress.utexas.edu/index.php/rp-form

First paperback edition, 2014

TO MISS IMA HOGG

She had the vision to see, a quarter century
ago, the need for school social work and
backed that vision with moral and
financial support.

CONTENTS

That Lonesome Road

There is an old song that goes, "Look down, look down, that lonesome road, before you travel on." Faced with nothing but that lonesome road, the adult might travel on. The child can't.

During my twenty-year career as a school social worker, I have dealt with two thousand children who faced that lonesome road. Problem children they are called. Presented here are a few cases selected from the two thousand.

There is only one common denominator among the children who walk alone—tragedy. It may be temporary, it may be permanent, depending usually on the manner in which worthwhile relationships with interested adults are established. Otherwise there is no pattern. The child may be unusually bright or barely above the level of a moron. He may be belligerent and destructive or withdrawn. He may be from a broken home or from a home that people consider happy. He may be from the slums or from Middle America. He may be from a deprived ethnic group—blacks and Mexican-Americans—or from dominant Anglos.

There is usually a difference in the nature of the problem at different economic levels. There is a still greater difference if an ethnic minority is involved. And if a language barrier is added, then solving the problem might seem hopeless. Such a language barrier exists in the area in which I worked—South Texas. This barrier extends from the Gulf of Mexico to the Pacific, for that area is the Great Barrio—the land in which the barrio is the equivalent of black ghettos in many other parts of the nation.

Yes, we have black ghettos in Texas. But my experience with black children has been limited, as I will explain later. About half my cases have been with Mexican-Americans. Probably 46 percent of the remainder have been with Anglos. In recent years, I worked with a few black children. When I started my career in Texas, in 1947, few Mexican-American children went to school, and most of those who did were taught in little frame shacks called "Mexican schools." Few blacks went to school, and they were taught in equally flimsy shacks called "Negro schools." Blacks were barred from "our" schools by law. Mexican-Americans were barred by the freezeout policy.

All this is changing rapidly—and it pleases me that I could be an active party to the process of change for twenty years. However, one should not be deceived as to extent of change, as indicated by the fact that, as recently as 1969, only 11 percent of Mexican-American children in Texas finished high school. The school structure, with one or two notable exceptions that may be only temporary, is Anglo dominated, even in cities where far more than half the population is Mexican-American. And there is a tendency, an inevitable part of the human attitude, I presume, to enforce the squeezout, easeout, kickout policy more vigorously when a Mexican-American or a black child causes problems.

Roughly, my work can be divided into two phases. First, blocking attempts at freezeout, squeezout, and kickout. Second, trying to see that the problem child had a chance to solve his problems and advance within the limits of his ability. It has not been easy, for the easeout policy extends on down to the classroom teacher. I do not unload blame on her, for her teaching is often evaluated largely on the basis of her ability to put on display a class of thirty quiet, obedient children when the principal, curriculum supervisor, or other judge makes his observations.

Pressures often cause teachers to try to shift problem children to other classrooms, and I have seen this practice carried to fantastic extremes—a bright-eyed, enthusiastic young teacher launching her career and discovering, to her dismay, that she has almost an entire room of problem children. They were unloaded on her by older teachers who had "adjusted" in the interest of survival.

Sure, I have a big advantage over the classroom teacher in dealing with children because I talk with them individually or in quite small groups. The classroom teacher can not. She must deal with them en masse. So I have enjoyed all of my relationships with problem children—even though many have been exhausting and painful at times to classroom teachers.

But I face problems that the teacher does not face. It is a joy to listen to a little child, for the child is a truly original, creative person—his mind has not set into a pattern. It is no pleasure facing angry parents and other relatives and angry teachers and administrators and angry probation officers. It is a battle all the way down the line. I never see a child unless someone has failed. It may be the child himself, the teacher, the principal, the parents, or any combination thereof. And it is only natural that the tides of emotion run high when it is clear that someone has failed. But if the problem child is to be saved, someone *must* battle.

I regret only one thing—that I decided to take leave, after the 1969–70 school year, just as the Chicano movement was taking definite form, the Mexican-American *demanding* his rights instead of begging for them. I would like to be a party to the school operation today, since I would not feel as lonesome and hopeless as I did many times in the past when I faced the school structure in trying to defend a Chicano.

But there are other compensations—presenting these cases, for example. All cases are factual. All names have been changed and the school districts are not identified. The objective in presenting these cases is to show what has happened—and possibly encourage others to work for improvement.

Hart Stilwell, my husband, wrote the final version of this book. But it is my story, so it is told in the first person.

ANNE STILWELL
Austin, Texas

THE CHILD WHO WALKS ALONE

Spider Legs

Barbara lived too far from school to go home for lunch unless she made the round trip at a brisk run. And she knew what her tired, sick mother would tell her if she got home in time to eat a few quick bites. "Go in the kitchen and get yourself some bread and molasses," her mother would say.

Molasses hurt Barbara's teeth. She hated it. But the school people told her to pay the full twenty-five cents for the cafeteria lunch or go home at noon. Barbara had been cut off the partial-pay lunch program—fifteen cents instead of twenty-five—because Miss Prentice, her classroom teacher, had caught her chewing bubble gum that she had bought for a nickel. "If you can afford to buy bubble gum, you can afford to pay for your food," Miss Prentice said.

Barbara's father didn't have any money that week. In his younger days he had been a cedar chopper in the hill country near Austin, capital city of Texas. Now he used his ancient truck to drive around and collect junk, which he sold—or tried to sell.

A child learns techniques of satisfaction, even though they may be vicarious, that few adults understand. Barbara learned that, if she ran fast all the way home and spent only a minute or so pretending that she was eating bread and molasses, by running fast all the way back to the school she could reach the cafeteria in time to watch the others eating their dessert. Maybe not the children, for they ate in a hurry so they could get out on the playground. But some teachers would be eating.

The thin little eight-year-old would sit and watch. She watched the food on the table—the jello that shook a bit when touched and was almost irresistible, the ice cream that caused her mouth to water after the manner of Pavlov's dogs. Some teacher might eat pie à la mode, and Barbara would fix her gaze on the eating process. She watched the spoon or fork move as it picked up a bite, watched the food being put into the mouth of the teacher, then watched the jaws working. Her jaws worked in unison. Her mouth watered more.

When all the teachers had finished eating, Barbara would wander out to the playground, hungry and a little weak. She didn't play with the other children. She watched. It seemed that much of her life was spent that way—watching. Gorky's "Bystander."

Barbara is, in a way, a name out of the past. I had been in school social work only a few years when I was called in to see if I could help the teacher and the principal deal with her. "She is sullen and disrespectful," the teacher said. "She could do much better if she made any effort, but she doesn't. And she distracts other children from their work, especially with that bubble gum."

This was in the days when bubble gum was a novelty, and I could understand the classroom reaction when some child blew a Grade A bubble—then maybe let it bust. "Does she blow bubbles in class quite often?" I asked Miss Prentice.

"Well, I've caught her only twice," the teacher said, as though regretting the minor nature of her achievement. "But she's been getting the twenty-five–cent lunch for only fifteen cents, and if she can afford to pay a nickel for bubble gum, she can afford to pay for her lunch. And she misbehaves," Miss Prentice quickly added when she noticed the expression on my face as I reflected on that squandered nickel of taxpayers' money.

"When a child, especially a quiet little girl such as Barbara, misbehaves, she is probably trying to tell you something by her actions that she is unable to tell you in words," I suggested. "I will try to find out and talk to you again."

"They're all, the whole family, just poor white trash . . ." Miss Prentice started, then checked herself. The expression "poor white trash" is dying out in Texas, probably because of the tendency of whites generally to join forces against the rising tide of black and Chicano protest. But Miss Prentice, who was well along in years, could not easily abandon a phrase so expressive as "poor white trash."

"I will talk to Barbara and her parents," I said.

First I talked to the child. She was sullen and unresponsive, just as Miss Prentice had said. But the attitude of an eight-year-old child can be changed, in most cases, by an intelligent adult who is genuinely interested. "Why do you chew bubble gum in class?" I asked.

"I don't," Barbara said.

"Miss Prentice said she saw you twice."

No response.

"Do you like to chew the gum or just blow bubbles?"

"My teeth don't hurt so much when I chew it," she said.

"Sometimes at home I have to eat molasses when we don't have anything else and it hurts my teeth. Bubble gum stops the hurting."

In those days, at the beginning of my career, there were practically no arrangements set up by the school systems and the community for such things as free dental care for children.

I got little information from Barbara during that first conference. I told her I would try to get her back on the reduced-pay lunch program and suggested that she do her bubble-gum chewing outside the classroom. "At least don't blow any real big bubbles in class," I said. The little child smiled—we were getting through to each other.

Then I visited the home. The mother was hanging clothes on the line—and complaining. After several visits I concluded that she spent a major part of life hanging clothes on the line and complaining. "I ought not be working like this," she said. "The doctor told me with my high blood pressure I ought not stand on my feet too much. My feet swell up. See?" She pointed to her feet. They were swollen. "But with Barbara and them five younger ones it's just work, work all the time."

Then Jim Houston, the father, drove his ancient truck into the yard and entered the house. He was a thin, worn little man with pale blue eyes and a defeated look. He appeared to be about fifty-five but was probably ten or twelve years younger. He was, in a way, a remnant of a once vigorous, proud pioneering people, the Anglos who first settled the hill country near the state capital. But, like many of the original Anglo settlers of the huge Big Thicket in East Texas, these people and their descendants clung to a way of life long after it had ceased to fit into the general pattern.

Jim Houston had been a cedar chopper in his younger days, and he was proud to be a third-generation cedar chopper even though he chopped no cedar. Owning your own land and chopping cedar for fence posts had been a proud way of life. And the fact that chopping cedar is a fiendish task—the goo comes out of the tree and sticks to the axe—made the cedar choppers even prouder. But life for the cedar choppers began to turn sour not long after the beginning of the present century. Cedar was running short. Ranchers were finding cheaper substitutes. And along came the power saw, which cedar choppers hated as much as oil well roughnecks hated the metal hat when it first showed up— and early-day football players hated the helmet.

There was a strange interlude of precarious prosperity during the Prohibition era, when cedar choppers learned that they could reap a rich harvest by turning the peaches they grew into whiskey. For years the peach whiskey of the hill country near Austin was as famous as the white lightning of the Big Thicket. That faded. Then men called developers bought up the land of the cedar choppers, paying what the men on the soil considered fabulous prices. The big man-made lakes furnished the impetus —fish replaced cedar posts and peach whiskey.

So the onetime cedar choppers began wandering into Austin. Most of them had one thing in common—they would not work for wages. No man could boss them. They had pride. Some became successful in various ways—the law, education, business, engineering. Some, like Jim Houston, were simply defeated. But he still clung to his "pride." He would work for no man.

It was a bit ironical watching that "pride" fade when I suggested that I might get Barbara on the free lunch program—no pay at all. I tried. And failed. But I did manage, after Barbara promised that she would not buy any more bubble gum, to get her back on the partial-pay program—fifteen cents for lunch.

Every day she showed up at school with a nickel and a dime. And after several more conferences and the passage of weeks, I began to be hopeful. Even the stony face of Miss Prentice seemed to relax when we discussed Barbara. "She is doing some better,"

Miss Prentice said. "The child is bright enough to make good grades. And she has stopped distracting other children." Then she added a comment that puzzled me for a moment. "But she turns up her nose at some of the food on the cafeteria lunch, food that she gets . . ."

"At taxpayers' expense," I cut in. Her face turned stony again, the thin lips tightened. But I simply could not endure hearing her make that remark again.

"It *is* taxpayers' money," she said angrily.

"I know, I know," I said. "All ten cents of it. I'm trying to help this child—trying to save her. She has known nothing but poverty and sadness . . . a lonely little thing trying to communicate . . ." I stopped there, for I saw that the stony cast on the hard old face was not changing. And I decided I would check into the chances of having Barbara transferred to another classroom teacher.

"Miss Prentice says you don't eat all the food on the cafeteria lunch," I told Barbara at our next conference. "She thinks you should, since you pay only fifteen cents."

"They've got beets every day—beets, beets, beets," the child said. "They hurt my teeth real bad. I hate them. And Miss Prentice sits and watches me, and if I don't eat the beets, she says, 'You're getting them on charity and you ought to be glad to eat them.' Jean doesn't eat beets and Miss Prentice doesn't say anything to her."

Jean's father was a member of the school board.

"And when Miss Prentice sits close to me and watches me, I look at the big blue veins on her hands and I think they are spider legs and I get scared."

"Spider legs?"

"Yes, ma'am. I'm real scared of spiders. We get some in our house and I run outside when I see one. Those big blue veins on her hands . . . they're like spider legs . . . I'm afraid of them . . . I can't eat . . ."

This situation was far worse than I had thought. There was no longer any doubt—I had to get the child transferred, which wasn't easy to do then, and isn't exactly easy to do now. Before I could do anything, disaster struck. Miss Prentice told Barbara to come to her desk when the other children left for the cafeteria at noon. Barbara knew why. She sat cold, terrified, fingering a thin dime, which was all she had. No nickel. She knew what facing Miss Prentice would be. "Where is the nickel? Let me see the nickel..." and on and on.

Barbara had weakened, because her teeth were hurting so much, and had bought a stick of bubble gum. Jean had informed. So when the noontime bell rang, Barbara darted out of the room and raced home. Then she raced back . . . without eating lunch. As she ran toward the building a ball being used by other children in a game rolled toward her. She picked it up, intending to throw it back to the children. Then a window in the nearby school building caught her attention and she stood transfixed. The window had been cracked. Someone had thrown a small stone against it, not big enough to shatter the glass, but big enough to make a little spot out from which radiated cracks in a crazy pattern— in all directions. As Barbara stared at the irregular lines they suddenly became spider legs . . . like the veins on Miss Prentice's hands.

I walked out of the cafeteria at that moment, in time to see Barbara hurl the ball through the window, shattering the glass. I grabbed her and held her close to me, trying to calm her.

"I killed it!" she said hysterically. "It was spider legs . . . Miss Prentice's hands . . . it was the blue veins . . . the spider legs . . . I killed the spider legs . . ."

I took her into my office and quieted her.

All quibbling about procedure was a thing of the past. I was going to see that this child had a chance in life. I took her home then went to the principal. He was a kindly man but not of a strong character. Perhaps that combination was fortunate, for, even though he was frightened at the thought of making any break with procedure, he was more frightened by the picture of disaster that I painted for him. He agreed to have Barbara transferred . . . and no conference with Miss Prentice. And he agreed not to charge Barbara's father for the broken window, since a replacement order had already been made after the earlier crack.

I had Barbara transferred to the classroom of a teacher I knew was competent. She was firm but she was kindly and reasonable. And she was patient. Patience is probably the greatest single virtue a teacher can have. I talked quite a bit to Mrs. Knight, the new teacher, before taking Barbara to her class. "The child has had a rough life any way you look at it," I said. "She has pride, a sort of family or clan pride even though her people are so poor they can't pay the full price for her lunch. Her father spent most of his early years as a cedar chopper . . ."

"Cedar chopper!" Mrs. Knight broke in.

"Yes. Her ancestors all down the line were cedar choppers."

"We will go right out to her home this afternoon and look into this," Mrs. Knight said.

"Why?"

"Because I am from a long line of cedar choppers. I want to meet her people. We might even be distant kinfolks."

And so we went to Barbara's home, and the pale blue eyes of the little cedar chopper father shone brightly as he and Mrs. Knight talked about their people. They knew most of the cedar chopper "heroes" of earlier days, when working cedar with an ax sometimes reached the level of an art.

Suddenly some bright colors penetrated the gloom that had been Barbara's life. "She is doing just fine—a bright, happy little girl," Mrs. Knight told me. "And things are going to be still better. I've got a cedar chopping cousin who's a dentist, and he's going to work on her teeth for free—us cedar choppers stick together. About that bubble gum—I keep a couple of sticks of it in my desk to give her whenever she wants one. But we have a deal—no bubble blowing in class."

I moved to Houston soon after the end of the school year. And at Christmas time I got a card from Barbara. "I am not afraid of spider legs any more," the child scrawled. "Mrs. Knight told me not to be."

And at the bottom of the card was a note from Mrs. Knight. "Us cedar choppers are doing real fine. Thanks again for saving a lonely little girl."

I didn't save Barbara. Mrs. Knight did. But I had a nice, warm feeling inside for days just thinking about that card.

Ramon's Bicycle

And so, like the little boys in blue in that old Sam Hall ballad, the police they came too. They had no choice—they were, in line of duty, answering a call from the school. And they took away Ramon's bicycle. When they did, they took away half of Ramon's life. The other half, music, came on the air waves and nobody could take that away.

The principal and the physical education instructor and two other men on the faculty of Travis Junior High surrounded Ramon's bicycle and held it captive until the police arrived. Ramon had been suspended from school again, and it was against regulations for him to ride his bicycle on school grounds while he was suspended. He rode it on school grounds, and the four men captured it.

Ramon could get his bicycle back if his mother went to the police station with him. But this was Tuesday and his mother was at work. She couldn't go until Saturday. Ramon's father couldn't go, because he was serving a term in the state penitentiary for possession of marijuana. Ramon's older brothers couldn't go, because they were in the state correctional school.

The four men who captured the bicycle were baiting the thin, thirteen-year-old Mexican-American boy—laughing at his humiliation and confusion—when I approached the school. I avoided them. A school social worker should maintain self-control. There are situations in which I can maintain self-control only by walking away. I walked away.

At best, life for Ramon was a meager thing. In his opinion there was no hope. "I've got three strikes against me and I'm out," he told me when I went to the tiny family home the first time he was suspended. "I'm a Mexican, I don't have a father, and I've been kicked out of school. And I wanted to stay and play my guitar and sing in the talent contest. If I win I might get started . . ."

"Will you play your guitar for me?" I asked, nodding toward the instrument. I had heard him playing it when I approached the home. He was "sitting in" with music coming on the radio. He had turned the radio off and put the guitar in a corner when I entered.

In order to see Ramon when he was not in school, I had to go in the morning, during his music period. The afternoon was dedicated to his bicycle, the other half of his life. On the bicycle he could zip along, feeling as free as the cowboy of the Old West. Of course the bicycle liberated Ramon from nothing, except in his own mind at the moment, just as riding the plains on a horse did not change the status of the oldtime cowboy, an underpaid hired hand. But both felt free, and a human being is pretty much what he feels that he is.

Ramon played and sang a couple of songs. I was pleased by his technical proficiency and delicate touch. And the small voice was pure, the phrasing interesting. "Did you take lessons?" I asked.

"No ma'am. I learned from the radio."

"Will you sing a huapango for me?" I asked.

A puzzled expression came over the attractive, swarthy Spanish-Indian face, and he looked at me as though he did not understand. I am a blue-eyed Anglo. I can't even pronounce the word *enchilada* correctly. So why should I ask Ramon to sing a huapango, the most interesting and authentic of Mexican folk songs. "But . . . you don't know any Spanish, do you?" Ramon said.

"My husband plays the guitar and sings huapangos," I explained. "He grew up along the Rio Grande and knows Spanish. But he doesn't play and sing nearly as well as you do. You sound like some of the fine professional musicians we have heard in Mexico."

The boy's face glowed. Suddenly I became a different person, someone with whom he might communicate. In the past he had grudgingly accepted me because I seemed to be the only Anglo interested in his problems.

And so Ramon sang the huapango and it was lovely. He had talent. This boy would win the talent contest. And winning might start him on a different path in life, especially since he had a friend who had agreed to give him a tryout with a small group if he won. There was small chance that he could ever go far in any other line of endeavor, especially one geared to a high school graduate's level. For those who ran the school structure in that particular San Antonio suburb were not willing to make any more "concessions," as they termed them, to Ramon. He had passed the easeout, squeezeout phases and was now ready for the kickout.

But in the world of music . . . ah, what a difference. It goes over and under and around and through barriers. And a boy with talent might pull himself out of the barrio and avoid the gloomy prospects of correctional school, followed, possibly, by prison. Louis Armstrong "survived" reform school and went on to speak, with his horn, a beautiful language that broke all barriers and became international. Few others do.

Ramon had been suspended for making insulting remarks about the physical education instructor. The remarks were made on the playground. I never learned what Ramon said, and I probably wouldn't have understood if I had been told. For even though there was, at that time, a rule against the use of Spanish anywhere on the school grounds, Mexican-American boys— Chicanos, as they are now generally called—were likely to use some choice epithet in Spanish to express contempt for a faculty member and you don't learn those epithets in high school Spanish.

Not more than 5 percent of all the Anglo teachers in the greater San Antonio area actually have a working use of Spanish, even though more than half the total population (not counting military establishments) is Mexican-American. But most of the Anglo men are familiar with those insulting comments in Spanish. Ramon uttered one, so out he went. And he couldn't come back until he apologized to the physical education instructor and "took his licks."

"I will not take any licks from him," Ramon told me. "Or from anybody else."

"Hasn't anything good ever happened to you?" I asked.

"Nothing," he said. "All has been bad."

"How about the guitar and the radio and the bicycle?"

"They're good," he admitted. "But if I can't play my guitar and sing in the talent contest, what's the use?"

"Could you make it if your father were here, even though he is Mexican-American?" I asked.

"Sure. They'll listen to a man when he takes his boy back to school, but they won't listen to my mother."

I had learned that the freezeout technique was being applied in this case. It is a follow-up to suspension—a procedure guaranteeing that the boy won't get back in school even though the board might never officially expel him. The principal, or perhaps the assistant principal, to whom disciplinary matters are often delegated, makes it almost impossible for the parent of the unwanted boy to follow the requirements. The mother must bring the boy to school. He must apologize and take his licks. Ramon's mother tried, even though it meant taking off from work and losing a day's pay. The assistant principal had a way of being out or being busy. She went once without Ramon. No deal. She had to produce a warm, delinquent body.

"Could you make it if you were an Anglo?" I asked the boy.

"Sure I could, even not having a father. An Anglo boy can make it. This is *his* country."

"Could you make it if I got you back in school?"

"I would try," he said. "Yes, I think I could . . . I want to play my guitar." Then he added, as an afterthought, "But no licks. Nobody beats me."

"All right, one good thing is going to happen to you," I said. "I am going to get you back in school."

After I left I wondered what had prompted me to make that promise. As a social worker I had battled school structures in various parts of Texas for twenty years. I knew how grudgingly those structures yield, which is probably necessary within certain limits, since no operation so vast can function without a structural pattern. But I had also learned that this apparently immovable object *will* yield to an irresistible force. I would be just that . . . I would move the immovable object or join Ramon in the ranks of the kickouts. I had too much "invested" in this boy now—too much to back off and let him follow the path of his father and brothers.

There had been the running battle of the eye glasses. Ramon's eyesight was so poor that he was reprimanded one time for "loitering in the halls," when all he was doing was trying to read the numbers above the classroom doors to see where he should go. Several times I got him glasses—took him across town and got some charitable agency (Anglo, of course)—to have him fitted with glasses. Invariably he broke them . . . or "they got broke." Maybe he was venting his hostility on the Anglo charitable agency that gave him the glasses. As a friend of mine once remarked, "No good deed ever goes unpunished." Anyway, the glasses episodes were just part of my struggle to keep the boy out of the penitentiary . . . and maybe help him on to a good life in an art form, music.

By sheer coincidence, a member of the school board, a Mexican-American, came to the rescue. I seldom have any contact with school board members. But suddenly I formed quite an admiration for that particular school board member.

He had noticed Ramon riding his bicycle during school hours and talked to the boy. He got the story, including the part about the talent contest and what it might mean in launching Ramon on a career in music. He phoned the principal, and the principal got in touch with me and asked me to bring Ramon back to school.

"He says he won't take any licks from the physical ed. instructor," I warned.

"He won't have to take any licks," the principal said.

I went and got Ramon and led him by the hand, back into school. And as we were walking along the hall the physical education instructor noticed us and stepped out. "What's going on here?" he demanded.

"I'm bringing him back to school," I said.

"Not before he takes his licks."

"You talk to the principal about that," I said, and moved on.

So Ramon was back in school, practicing on his guitar way into the night and zipping along on his bicycle in late afternoon and early evening. Rush traffic after five o'clock was a challenge he loved. He maneuvered through it as an oldtime cowhand maneuvered through the mesquite trees of South Texas.

All fine. But it didn't last. It couldn't. The physical education instructor was not going to accept defeat. So, without saying a word to me, the principal kicked Ramon out of school again. Same old charge—making insulting remarks about the physical education instructor. I still wonder if Ramon said anything. I doubt it. But I admit that he might have made one of the many suggestive and often insulting gestures used by Latin-oriented males. Maybe he merely held two fingers above the back of his head, and, as the Italian count said, "If I must wear horns on my head, may they be of velvet." And that time they took Ramon's bicycle away.

Okay, the irresistible force set out to move the immovable object. I barged into the office of the principal and asked if he was deliberately denying this deprived boy any chance to make it in life. "The talent contest is only two weeks from now," I said. "He's certain to win if the judges are fair. It could be a turning point in his life—to music instead of crime . . ."

The principal cut in. "We will not tolerate insults to school personnel. We will maintain discipline in this school."

"Would you like to guess how many insulting things the boys on the playground have said about you?" I asked.

"We will have discipline . . ."

"Even if it means condemning a boy to a hopeless life, probably a life of crime? You know the example this school system has set for him—two older brothers in the state correctional institution."

"No boy is going to make . . ." And on and on.

"Does the physical education instructor hide some place and watch and listen?" I asked. "Or does he have a spy system?"

"We will not discuss the matter any more," the principal said, standing up to let me know that the interview was over.

"I think we *will* discuss it some more," I told him.

But hope seemed slim indeed. The principal's smug manner convinced me that he had talked to the superintendent and had the full support of the superintendent to enforce the prescribed discipline. I presumed it must be that way. That left only one hope—Ramirez, the school board member who had got Ramon back into school a few weeks earlier. Ramirez had done that on his own—not because of any urging by me. I am reluctant to approach a school board member. But . . . I was desperate.

That afternoon I did something I seldom do—talked to my husband about the problem. We have a general understanding that he handles his writing and I handle my social work and never the twain shall meet—except in this book. But I broke the rule. And, as I might have expected, my husband immediately came forth with a suggestion that shook me. As a social worker I am forced to operate within the structure. My husband has always operated within a structure of his own improvisation, and his structure is fluid, ranging, in my opinion, from frightening to terrifying.

"If you want to get Ramon in the band, it's simple," my husband said. Practically all his "simple" procedures are frightening to me.

"Tell me how," I said. "But tell me gently and slowly."

"Call Ramirez and get him to agree to bust the whole story at the board meeting tomorrow night. Have Ramon there with his guitar . . ."

"Are you crazy? Playing and singing at a school board meeting."

"Leadbelly sang his way out of prison," he said. "I'll call the city editor and I'm sure he will have a reporter and a camera man there. We'll make Ramon famous even if he doesn't get back in school."

See why I seldom mention my career problems in talking to my husband? At that time he was writing a column for a San Antonio newspaper. And there is no doubt that he could actually have got a photograph of Ramon, along with a story, in the paper. But how about me? I wouldn't even show up for work the following day. I'd mail in my resignation. "I'll have leaders of little groups in town bidding for him," my husband went on, delighted with his idea as he expanded it. I finally told him to stop. He wanted to know if I was afraid of losing my job. I said no, but quitting in a dopey way such as that . . .

"Okay, stick with your routine and see how far you get," he said.

"I will call Ramirez tomorrow," I finally said.

"Call him now. Why wait?"

"I prefer to call during school hours."

I called the next morning—and have regretted from that day to this that I did not take my husband's advice and call Rameriz the previous afternoon, for when I called it was too late. "Haven't you heard?" Ramirez asked, surprised.

"Heard what?"

"Ramon was run over last night . . . he was riding a bicycle . . . it was a busy street . . . dark . . ."

The way he said it told me that I need ask no more questions.

It would be wrong to say that Ramon stole the bicycle, for he was not a thief. He borrowed the bicycle, intending to return it. A friend rode Ramon, on the friend's bicycle, around until they located a bicycle that Ramon could "borrow" to go for a ride. The friend told me the story, and assured me that Ramon was going to return the bicycle.

On his own bicycle Ramon was a genius at weaving in and out of traffic, even at night. But the bicycle he had borrowed was strange to him, just as a different guitar would have been strange. The pedals, the seat, the handlebars, the brakes—all were different. He didn't maneuver it very well. Yet he was driven by an irresistible compulsion to get on a bicycle and zip along, feeling the breeze on his face—feeling free! And since his own bicycle had been captured and taken away, he borrowed another. He *had* to have his hour of freedom.

"I saw bright sparks on the pavement where his bicycle was dragged by the car," the boy with Ramon told me. "It dragged the bicycle a long way."

And so Ramon died. And there will be discipline on the school playground.

I Want to Be a Polar Bear

Judy, age ten, black and almost completely isolated in a white-brown world, was accomplished at three things: fighting, running, and singing. There wasn't enough room in my office for running, and I wasn't interested in promoting fights. So I said sing. Judy sang.

A teacher stuck her head in the door and said, "When did you start giving singing lessons?"

"Today," I said. "Want to join? Might do you good."

"No thanks," she said and left.

I was curious about possible reaction in offices and classrooms nearby, for when Judy sang, loose objects in the room trembled. Let the others wonder. I had a job to do, and a school social worker often plays it by ear—or not at all. Judy sang it by ear.

She sang "Yellow Bird." The lyrics tell of a bird trapped in a cage, and as the black child sang she was telling me that she was trapped in a cage. My job was to open the cage. Judy really let herself go when she sang a spiritual made famous by Mahalia Jackson. The little child's eyes shone—I thought I detected a gleam of hope. It changed to bitterness as she sang a savage parody of "Summertime." She substituted wintertime for summertime. The going was rough, not easy. The cotton was low, not high. And the daddy was ugly, not good looking. She was telling me in songs what she had not been able to communicate in conversation.

When I was called in on the case, Judy was a wild creature. She sank her teeth into the fleshy part of the principal's hand, and hung on, bulldog style, until he beat her on the head with a clipboard. She fought with any child, boy or girl, who would stand still. Most wouldn't. They had learned to take flight, for Judy was large for her age and was a grade behind in school. Others in her classroom were no match for her. And she was constantly belligerent, which is not unusual. Most blacks with pride tend to become belligerent when the routine defenses used by whites fail to serve. The child also was openly defiant, but that meant I had something solid to work with. Few things are more frustrating than a child who is defeated and has withdrawn from the active stream of life.

"She doesn't belong in the public schools," Mrs. Wilkins, the classroom teacher, assured me when I was called in. "It's not right to inflict a wild hyena like that on other children. She should go to a private school where they can beat some discipline into her."

"What private school would you suggest?" I asked.

"I don't care just so they get her out of here."

"Her step-father has four children of his own," I said. "On an army sergeant's pay, how could he support them and send Judy to a private school? And I ask you again, what private school?"

"Send her to the reform school," the teacher said, ignoring the fact that sending a ten-year-old girl to the state correctional school would be a quite extraordinary procedure.

When you work in multiethnic school systems as long as I have, you learn to detect race prejudice even when circumstances seem not to justify it. Mrs. Wilkins was from Illinois, graduate of a first-rate university. It was difficult to believe that part of her hostility toward Judy was racially motivated. But I had worked with her on cases involving some Anglo and Mexican-American children who were pretty wild, and I detected a difference in her attitude toward Judy.

I talked to the principal about it. "She would die rather than admit it," he said, "but she is prejudiced against Negroes." And this principal was a veteran administrator of sound judgment. I felt a bit proud of him for coming, indirectly, to the defense of Judy, especially since his left hand was still bandaged as a result of the tooth wounds.

"What is your idea of procedure?" I asked. "I doubt if I can do much in the present atmosphere."

"It seems that we have three choices," he said. "Suspend Judy from school, and I don't want to do that—at least until this wound heals." He held up his bandaged hand and managed a smile. "We could transfer her to another classroom and hope. Or keep her where she is and lose a teacher. Mrs. Wilkins has notified me that, if Judy doesn't go, she will."

"I'm glad the decision is yours, not mine," I said.

"You don't get out that neatly," he said. "I'll transfer her— but *you* pick the new teacher."

He had me. The decision was mine after all. But . . . that's what I was getting paid for, so I started the search for a teacher for Judy.

Meantime I had another conference with the child and learned that she had another talent. First she blasted out "No More Cane on the Brazos," a folk song made famous by Odetta. Then she did a little drawing. It interested me, so I got out some drawing paper and crayolas that I kept on hand and Judy began really drawing. The child had talent! No doubt in the world about it. "Come on, let's go show these to the principal," I said.

"*No* . . . I bit him . . ."

She was terrified, but I finally persuaded her that the principal would not harm her. In fact, he was delighted by the drawings. "Fine, just fine," he said. "I'll have some of these put up on the walls in the hallway . . . and put your name on them, Judy." The child was walking a foot above the floor as we left.

The first step. Build the child's confidence in herself. Then it might not be necessary for her to prove it by beating other children. "I'm going to make a lot more drawings, and maybe they'll put them all up on the classroom walls," Judy said.

"Sure. But Judy, can you try to get along better with other children and with the teacher . . ."

"Mrs. Wilkins hates me," she cut in.

Adults *think* they keep emotional reactions secret from children. They don't. The child can sense adult hostility as easily as a dog scents human fear.

"We're going to put you in a different classroom," I said.

"A different teacher!!!"

"Yes. You'll have what people used to call a 'clean slate.' That means a fresh start like you have in races."

"I promise to quit fighting," she said. "I won't fight anybody any more. I'll behave and show you what a nice girl I can be."

It was only a promise, emotionally inspired. And if you expect sudden transformation of a human personality after the manner of the "miracles" you see on such TV shows as *Room 222*, then you are living in a lovely dream world. I had to live in the world of reality.

I have had little experience with black children. Integration of blacks into the general school structure in Texas was little more than a subject of conversation until 1965 or later. And segregation is still a reality in many school districts because of residential segregation. So in the San Antonio surburban district where I worked for five years, there were practically no blacks. The few black children in the system were there because of gradual changes in employment policies at the nearby military establishments.

Judy was one of the first black children with whom I had dealt, and I was particularly anxious not to fail in this new challenge. I shopped around carefully and found a teacher, a Mrs. Mohle—third-generation Texan of German extraction—who I felt certain would give the little girl a chance.

A lot of things began falling in line quickly. Judy's big need was in spelling, Mrs. Mohle told me. So at each of our weekly conferences I would follow Judy's singing session with a lesson in spelling. And Judy, evidently deeply appreciative, began listening to the rules that Mrs. Mohle enforced—no playing in the mud, no "rain baths" when it was raining, no loud noises in class and so on. "My mother wouldn't care if I did any of those things," Judy told me.

"Your mother doesn't have thirty other school kids in a class with you," I said. "And you might catch cold, then your parents would blame the teacher. Anyway, do you want to muddy up the classroom?"

"I guess not," she said, but added, "My mother wouldn't care."

I had already learned, during several visits to the home, that the mother's attention was devoted almost constantly to the four younger children, and she had little time to worry about Judy.

Then Mrs. Mohle dropped by my office one day, and it was easy to see that she was in high spirits. "Judy stood aside and let another girl, a smaller one, move ahead of her in the lunchroom line," she said. "And I was watching when she did the same thing on the playground when the children were playing ball. She's trying real hard. But she still gets into fights."

"I guess because all the white-and-brown world around her seems hostile."

"The other children do say things," Mrs. Mohle agreed. "I hear a remark now and then. But you can't stop that."

"At least not as long as they hear those things at home," I said.

At my next conference with Judy I asked if she would like to have another girl from her class join in our little session. For a moment she didn't answer. I saw her frown and touch her forehead. "What's the trouble?" I asked.

"My step-father hit me on the head with a big kitchen spoon," she said. "It hurts when I touch it."

"Why did he hit you?"

"Because I wasn't washing dishes fast enough."

"Maybe you'd better wash faster—the way you run."

She grinned then checked the grin quickly—the wrinkles hurt her forehead. But there was nothing I could do about Judy's home life. I had checked carefully. I got no reaction from the father . . . I, another blue-eyed white, intruding into his life.

Her father, a career army sergeant, was proud of his stripes. Not many blacks had stripes—at least not that kind. He was proud even to the point of arrogance, which is not inconsistent with reality. As a famed black poet wrote many years ago, "When the Negro gets his freedom, he is going to walk hard and talk loud." Once the father had barged into the office of the principal and threatened to do bodily harm to him. But that was because of a younger child—his own. Not Judy. He had no interest in her. And Judy's mother wasn't a strong enough character to stand up to the disciplinarian. So little Judy didn't have exactly what you could call a rich life—and for compensation she ran fast and fought hard and sang loud.

She showed up at her next conference with a little friend, as I had suggested—but the girl was white, not black. I had taken it for granted that she would bring a black girl. But she breezed in with a blue-eyed blonde. Real fine! And the following week another Anglo girl.

So the school year was drawing to a close with prospects much brighter for Judy. "She still can't spell very well," Mrs. Mohle said.

"It would be a disaster to keep her in the same grade another year," I suggested. "She is already a year behind—and large for her age."

"Oh, I'm going to pass her," Mrs. Mohle said. "She spells ten times better now—couldn't spell at all until you started those lessons. And her conduct isn't bad. Just a minor flareup occasionally." Then she said, "If she just gets a sympathetic, understanding teacher in the fall ..."

"That's my job," I said. "Trust me."

Judy came to our last conference alone. At first she was jubilant. I knew why, but I waited for her to tell me. "At the track meet I ran faster than all the rest," she said. "I got a ribbon. See?"

"Wonderful," I said, fingering it.

Then she lapsed into a despondent mood. "What good does it do to run fast if you're dumb and can't spell?"

"You can learn to spell as easily as you learned to run."

"I didn't learn that," she said.

"Oh yes you did. You even had to learn to stand up and walk. Spelling isn't much different."

There was another lapse in the conversation, and again Judy seemed moodily reflective. Then for some reason, probably the centuries-old hope of black Americans to escape the cage, she turned to reincarnation. "What were you in your last reincarnation?" she asked.

I was too surprised to react immediately. "How do you happen to know about reincarnation?" I asked.

"I hear the grownups talking about it."

I stalled for time. "What were you before you became a human being?" I finally said, switching the burden to her.

"I can run fast, so I guess I was a horse."

"What color horse?" The time is past when such niceties as avoiding mention of colors are considered "proper" procedure in discussions between blacks and whites.

"A black horse," she said without hesitation.

"What do you want to be next time?"

"A polar bear."

A shiver ran through me. You do not ask what color polar bear. You do not ask why a lonely little black child in a white-brown world longs to be a polar bear.

"And I will have a polar bear husband and some polar bear babies and polar bear sisters . . ." She went on and on, fitting herself into this all-white polar bear world, getting more excited as she did. Then she insisted on knowing what I was the last go 'round.

"I guess I was a kitten," I said.

"What color kitten?"

"A yellow one."

"What do you want to be when you are reincarnated?"

"I'd like to be a kitten again."

"What color kitten?"

"I'll be yellow again." I admit I was afraid to say white.

"All right, I'll take you in when I am a polar bear and you can be my pet," Judy said. "And my polar bear husband and sisters and polar bear babies will all pet you and feed you and take care of you."

I felt tears forming in my eyes.

"Why are you crying?" Judy asked, puzzled.

I couldn't answer.

"We will take care of you and you will be our pet. You don't have to cry . . ."

Judy's step-father was transferred soon after that and I never saw her again. Now and then I think of her—and her polar bear family. In the mental picture I see Judy running faster and spelling better. And I hear her belting out "I am black and beautiful," not one of the degrading songs that black Americans sang for so many years . . . "I'm white, deep down inside, but I can't help this black spread all over my face."

Good Neighbor Policy

Janice Boles, age twelve, brain damaged and mentally retarded, menstruated once. Then a kindly neighbor baby-sitter, a man of forty-five, "stopped that bleeding nonsense," as the farm boy says in that ancient joke. This incident seemed to fit neatly into the pattern of tragedy interwoven in the lives of all members of the Boles family. They were what I call happenees—anything bad you could think of happened to them.

What happened to Janice might well serve as a warning to all parents of young girls. This case and many others quite similar to it clearly illustrate that the threat of rape of young girls, especially those not yet in their teens, is greater in the home than elsewhere. And quite often the threat is from middle-age or

elderly men rather than from youths. And, repulsive as it might
seem to many, high on the list of those mature and elderly males
who pose a threat are relatives—the father, an uncle, a grand-
father.

What do you do when a seven-year-old girl complains of pains
in her lower abdomen and investigation reveals that she is being
raped repeatedly by her father? You shudder and suppress an
urge to withdraw from the human race. I know—I was called in
on such cases.

The danger of some girl child being raped by a youth who lures
her with candy is not nearly as great as the threat of rape at
home by an older man. And if the sexual relationship continues,
which it frequently does if the father is the guilty adult, chances
of undoing the emotional damage to the child are not good.

The Boles family specialized in tragedy, as do many of the
families with whom I deal. Each tragedy seems to be a new twist
in a continuing pattern that can not be broken.

Janice Boles was badly brain damaged. Her father, later divorced by Mrs. Boles, dropped Janice on the sidewalk when she
was a baby. She fell on her head.

I was called in by the classroom teacher soon after the family
moved into our school district in South Texas. There were three
Boles children, Janice being the oldest. Examination showed the
brain damage, so I went to the home of the mother to get permission to place the child in a special education class. This permission was necessary in order to make the transfer.

Janice began getting along fairly well, considering her cap-
abilities. She had been toilet trained and was able to dress and
feed herself. She could learn in a quite elementary way. "She is
actually learning how to read!" Miss Sherman, the special education teacher, told me after she had worked with the child for
several weeks. "And she can add a few numbers. I think she

might eventually learn some skill, some simple handicraft, and maybe she will be able to support herself and be a contributing member of society instead of a lifelong burden."

But all was not serene on other fronts. It never is when I work with a whole "clutch" of problem children. Mrs. Walton, a teacher who had Ricky Boles in her room, soon began demonstrating hostility toward him and the rest of the family. Ricky was the youngest child, in second grade. Eva, two years older, was in the fourth grade. They were not bright children, yet they could pass and they caused no trouble. That is, they caused no trouble until I put the three children on the free lunch program. "It's outrageous, putting that family on the free lunch program while the father loafs around at home all the time," Mrs. Walton said.

"He's the step-father," I reminded her.

"Step-father, father, who cares. He's at home doing nothing."

"He is an out patient from the state mental hospital," I gently reminded her, trying to avoid open conflict.

"I don't care. They were in our church and we did everything possible to help them. Gave them food and clothes, got that lazy father job after job . . . and he never would work. Then when we cut off their dole they moved to another church. They've all got the gimmies. All they know how to do is hold out the hand. Now it's free lunches."

I didn't argue with Mrs. Walton because there was no need to. She had nothing to do with the free lunch program. I did. But I felt despondent about prospects for Ricky. How can a little seven-year-old who isn't particularly bright develop when his classroom teacher is frankly hostile? Tragedy in the home, tragedy at school.

Mrs. Boles, who was working in the cafeteria of the nearby military base when I first met her, unfolded the long, dreary story. Her first husband was a drunkard, she said. She divorced him and later married a "fine" man, one who didn't drink and didn't smoke and treated her and the children with affection. She even had the last name of the children legally changed to Boles so they wouldn't have to be reminded of their own "drunken" father. And Mr. Boles belonged to the church and went regularly with the family. But he turned out to be what Mrs. Boles called a weakling. He couldn't or wouldn't hold a job for any length of time. She had to work to support her children and, at times, her husband. The church people helped some. But when her husband did not stay long on any job, the church cut the family off.

The next time I saw her, three weeks later, Mrs. Boles had more bad news. Her husband's mother had died unexpectedly and he had gone into an emotional condition that persisted. He would sit—just sit. Sometimes he cried. Most of the time he stared into space, evidently not seeing. This withdrawal fit the pattern I had visualized from our previous conversations. The man had never broken the umbilical cord. "Untie the apron strings, Mama, they're choking me." Mama wouldn't untie the strings. And even death left the strings still binding.

The following week Boles's brother was killed in an automobile accident. It was too much. Boles went into a state of shock and was placed in the state mental hospital. And Mrs. Boles spent quite a bit of time with him, so many visits to the hospital that she finally lost her job at the cafeteria. I helped her fill out the forms required for welfare, and at the same time I had the children placed on the free lunch program at school.

Soon the husband was permitted to go home for short visits, then for longer ones. But he remained an out patient of the hospital and was not able to endure the strain of a job, no matter how elementary the work. And, in the opinion of Mrs. Walton and some others, the lazy man was just loafing . . . the family had the gimmies . . . the outstretched hand . . .

"I'm so thankful we have a real fine neighbor who helps us,"
Mrs. Boles told me on one visit when her husband was back in
the hospital for additional therapy. "I don't know how I would
get along without Mr. Whittaker."

"Who is he?" I asked.

"He lives next door, alone. He works at night, and when I go
to the hospital to visit Frank, he stays with the children. I don't
like to leave Janice, even with the other children. She's just like
a baby—almost helpless."

A warning sign flashed in my mind, but I didn't heed it,
mainly because I must guard against becoming an alarmist. You
can't carry on if you suspect the worst in all situations. But a
forty-five–year-old man, living alone, willing to spend his time
with three little children . . . I had an uneasy feeling. But I decided it would be dreadful to frighten Mrs. Boles, then find out
that there was no cause for alarm. I did ask a few questions.
"What do you know about Mr. Whittaker?"

"Oh, he's a real fine man—so kind. He belongs to our church.
I don't know what I'd do without him. And he brings the children
candy and other little gifts."

The bearer of gifts . . . the good neighbor. But I said no more.
I know of situations in which a man's life has been blighted—it
happened to a principal I once knew—by groundless suspicion.

"Frank will be home again tomorrow," the mother went on.
"And this time he might stay."

"I *sure* hope he does," I told her, and added, under my breath,
"for more reason than you might think."

The husband did stay home for two months and everything
seemed to be going along smoothly—that is, smoothly for the
Boles family. Then Mrs. Walton, again blocking my path in the
hallway as I walked toward my office, fired a new blast at the
family. I had to pass Mrs. Walton's room twice daily in going

to and from my office. Now and then she would waylay me and come out charging. "Free lunches!" she said with scorn. "And now they're getting a brand new color TV set. I'd like for you to explain that!"

"How do you know?"

"Ricky told me."

"Is the set already at their home?"

"Ricky said it's to be delivered today. I just thought you might like to know, since you got them on relief and the kids on the free lunch program."

"I'll check," I said, and walked on. I have never quite understood the resentment some people display when a deprived child is given lunch without charge. But I can assure you that there are plenty of people who put such resentment on display.

The next day when the final school bell rang, I was the one standing in the hall, waiting to intercept Mrs. Walton. "I'd like for you to make a little home visit with me," I said.

"I can't. I planned to go home early."

"I think you *can*," I said. "And I think you'd *better*. There are some things here that need clearing up once and for all."

She knew what I meant and she meekly followed me, in her own car, to the Boles home.

"This is Mrs. Walton," I told Mrs. Boles. "She is Ricky's classroom teacher and she has come to see your new color TV set."

Mrs. Boles sat and stared, bewildered. "New color TV . . . why I showed you that old broke-down black-and-white set my brother gave me . . ."

The "brand new" color set was a shopworn, dirty little black-and-white set. But the case had a mahogany finish, unlike the far dirtier ivory finish of the little set it replaced. So to Ricky, who had never watched color TV, it was a color set.

Mrs. Walton stared at the "color" set. "But Ricky . . . Ricky said . . ." she stumbled.

"A child who has little in life may want to make that little seem more important," I told her. "The case is color—mahogany."

"How is Ricky doing in school?" Mrs. Boles asked.

Mrs. Walton hesitated for a moment, switching her thoughts from color TV back to classroom. Then she said, "He's doing all right—just fine."

When Mrs. Walton and I walked back to our cars, she was still shaking her head. "I don't understand . . ." she mumbled.

"There are many things that those of us who have never lived in the slums or ghettos or barrios do not understand," I told her. "A teacher asked his class—all from the barrio—how many had air conditioners in their homes. Almost all raised their hands, to the astonishment of the teacher. But he soon realized the truth— the barrio children didn't know what air conditioning is. They thought fans were air conditioners. And to Ricky, the mahogany case made it a color TV."

"I'm sorry . . ."

Let her be sorry. It relieved me of static in this situation even though her attitude changed little. As for the family . . . well, I more or less presided over the dismemberment of the structure, even though Mr. Churchill refused to preside over the dismemberment of the Empire. He didn't have to—he got beat. I stayed on.

On my next visit I heard the sad news that Frank Boles, who had been suffering from a sore throat, had cancer and was to undergo surgery. Happenees, happenees. If he survived he might not be able to talk, Mrs. Boles said. Abandon hope all ye who enter here.

Several weeks later Mrs. Boles called me at the office, something she had never done before. I knew by the tone of her voice that tragedy had struck again. She asked if I would come to the home. I left immediately. "How is your husband?" I asked.

"He's getting well," she said. "He'll be able to talk, but not too good. They're sending him home from the hospital Saturday."

"Very fine."

"But I've got something a whole lot worse than that," she said. "You know when I was at the hospital with Frank a lot of the time, Mr. Whittaker would stay with the children. Baby-sit for them."

I braced myself. I knew what to expect, and even before she said it I felt a dreadful sense of guilt because I did not follow my first impulse and warn her.

"Ricky told me," Mrs. Boles said. "You know, when I would leave, that man . . . that Mr. Whittaker . . . would give Ricky and Eva a quarter apiece to go outside and play. He had Janice alone then . . ." She broke down and sobbed convulsively. "Oh my God, I don't know what to do," she moaned. "The poor little thing, only twelve, and she just menstruated one time. I took her to the doctor. The little thing is pregnant." The mother sobbed uncontrollably.

"I can find a good home for her not far from here," I told her. "You will be able to visit her often. And I can arrange for her to get special education there and arrangements for adoption of the baby could be made. We have problems like this many times, and we work them out."

I'm not sure she was hearing me. She kept repeating, "One little period in her whole life and now she's pregnant. And the poor little thing doesn't even know what happened. She just says the man hurt her a lot. She's like a little baby herself . . ."

"You could take the man into court and they'd put him away for twenty years," I told her.

"Oh God no!" she almost screamed. "We're going to leave. I've got to get away from here. I can't stand it any longer."

I understood. The mentally retarded girl and the two younger children would have to go into court and testify. I tried to put myself in the mother's position and decided that had Janice been my daughter I would not have endured the ordeal of putting the child on the stand.

Many child psychologists believe that forcing a little girl to get on the stand and describe the intimate details of the sex experience is even more damaging than what happened. Tends to create in the child a lasting fear of all sex. This may be one reason so few such cases come to light, especially if the guilty person is a relative, and even if the little girl is only six or seven years old. And if you wonder why this happens so often, you will have to dig deep into psychological analyses of abnormal sex behavior. However, some reasons are easy to understand—the child is there, available. And, as I mentioned, there is little danger of prosecution.

So Whittaker remained an untouchable. He could sit there and wait for another family to move in . . . another Janice . . . then take more candy and other gifts . . . the good neighbor.

I asked Mrs. Boles where she would go. She said to Laredo. This decision seemed strange, since about 90 percent of the 75,000 people at the Texas-Mexico border town are Mexican-Americans. And this blonde woman was going to take her blond brood there, where Spanish is spoken more than English. "I've got some friends there," Mrs. Boles explained. "They said they would help us."

I mentioned again the advisability of putting Janice in a nearby maternity home, but Mrs. Boles began showing signs of panic, so I said no more.

When she calmed down she said, "The reason I asked you to come here was to see if you would check the two younger children out of school," she said. "I want to see that it's done proper, so they won't have trouble at Laredo."

I told her I would handle it, and she said, fine, the family would leave Saturday as soon as her husband was brought home. And she made me promise that I would never say a word about what she told me. I haven't . . . until this day. I tell now because I know Mrs. Boles and Janice will not be hurt by the telling—but some other little girl child might be saved.

Pachuco with a Switchblade

The youth stared coldly at me, a faint suggestion of a smile on his face now and then as he so obviously enjoyed my state of fear. It was one of the few times in my career that I was in danger of physical harm. Or thought I was.

I was afraid to make a break for the open door. The youth could easily catch me, and he might start carving with that foot-long, razor-sharp switchblade knife. I knew the knife was razor sharp because I watched the blade slide through tough fingernails as though they were paper. He stood trimming his fingernails—for my benefit. Not from an aesthetic point of view, however, for as the knife slid through a nail he would look coldly at me again and maybe smile faintly. "See what it will do?" he was saying with that smile.

Juanita, age fourteen, sat on the sofa, her head bent down slightly. The youth, Pablo, was seventeen, a school dropout now on parole from what was then known as the state reform school. Pablo and the girl had come reluctantly out of the bedroom when I went to Juanita's home for the second time, after calling the juvenile probation officer. There was no point in speculating on what had been happening in the bedroom, for Pablo hadn't even bothered to put his shirt back on.

I noticed that his trousers were different from others I had seen. The top part was wide and pleated, then the trousers tapered down to cuffs so narrow I wondered how he was able to get his feet through them. I still hadn't made any connection between the odd trousers and the switchblade and the dread word *Pachuco*. I made the connection suddenly when I looked more carefully at his hands. On the left hand, just back of the place where thumb and forefinger joined, was a tatoo. It looked like the letter *Y* with a short diagonal line across it. The brand of a Pachuco. Each gang had its own tatoo.

I couldn't have made a dash for the door then. I couldn't even stand up any longer. I eased myself carefully down on the sofa beside Juanita, praying silently that the probation officer would suddenly show at the door and save me.

I had been warned about Pachucos. "They are mean, dangerous," the principal told me. "Stay away from them. They love to carve on people with switchblade knives. That's their specialty. You can tell them by the zoot suit and the ducktail hair and funny shoes and a tatoo mark on the hand, between thumb and forefinger."

The principal exaggerated a bit, I learned later, especially about that carving business. That took place mainly in fights between rival Pachuco gangs, although there was a dramatic but short period of savage knife wielding, involving many Anglos, during what came to be known as the Pachuco War near military bases in California. In Texas, I learned later when I checked into the situation—after the Pachuco era faded—there were practically no fights between Pachucos and Anglos.

Since I had never seen a Pachuco in the flesh, I paid little attention to the principal's warnings. Now as I watched one carefully grooming his fingernails with that vicious knife I was too weak to do anything—except talk. I did that. I kept a low monologue going, after the manner of a snake charmer tootling on his little woodwind gadget while a cobra weaves back and forth in front of his face. "Juanita will have a better chance in life if she stays in school . . . she can take some kind of vocational training . . . and the law says she must go to school . . . I just came here to tell her about the law . . ." On and on.

And all Pablo said was, "It doesn't make any difference. We're going to get married anyway."

"But until she is married . . ." I was saying. And I was thinking, "Come on probation officer. Come on mother. Rescue me." The probation officer had promised to bring Juanita's mother.

The minutes dragged. Now that Pablo had finished paring and smoothing off his fingernails, he began cleaning them. And cleaning . . . and cleaning . . .

The Pachuco movement, which reached a peak in the bloody Pachuco War, mainly in the San Diego area during World War II, came suddenly upon the scene a few years before the war and faded out gradually by 1955. It was a phenomenon that few Anglos understood. In fact, many Mexican-Americans did not understand it, just as many adult Anglos do not understand the current youth rebellion. And the Pachuco movement was basically a youth rebellion, one of the first in the history of our country. Today many people are inclined to argue that the Pachuco movement and the Chicano movement, which began to be a considerable factor in the life of the Southwest late in the 1960's, are basically the same. They are in some ways: Both were youth movements. And both were intitated by Mexican-Americans, now being referred to generally, by their own choice, as Chicanos.

But there was a great difference in one respect: The Pachuco movement was a protest against what the young Mexican-American considered a completely hopeless situation. There was no goal because there was no hope. So the objective was to withdraw, even from the Mexican-American socioeconomic structure. Withdraw and in one way or another release hostility. And the only reason there was little releasing of hostility against Anglos was that the Pachucos were part of an almost completely subjugated ethnic group, even though it constituted a large majority of the total population in many areas. Releasing hostility on Anglos was too dangerous.

The Chicano movement is entirely different, although in its early days many Anglos chose to dismiss it scornfully as another Pachuco movement. The Chicano has a goal—and he is *demanding* it. He wants full participation, as an equal, in the social and economic and political affairs of *his* nation. And he is seeking those goals by legal means, even though many Anglos choose not to apply the word to demonstrations, school boycotts, and so on. The Chicano has hope—and he is going to *make* that hope become reality.

The Pachuco was an outcast, even from his own ethnic group, with no hope—with nothing but hostility. He hated Anglos and was ashamed of his own people for meekly submitting to abuse. In isolating himself, even from his own ethnic group, the Pachuco established identity by his distinctive zoot-suit clothes, by the long, ducktail hair, by the switchblade, and by the tatoo.

Actually, the zoot suiter was the first longhair of modern times, and, of course, I am not speaking of classical musicians once scornfully referred to by jazz musicians as longhairs. Very amusing . . . now the rock and folk and country musicians are the longhairs.

Pachucos even developed a language of sorts, not particularly astonishing if you listen to a dedicated hippie or "head" and try to understand what he is saying. "I could listen for ten minutes as two Pachucos talked and I wouldn't understand what they were saying," Richard Moreno, chief of juvenile probation in San Antonio, told me in explaining the vast difference between the Pachuco and the Chicano.

Moreno had plenty of experience with Pachucos, for San Antonio was home base for two gangs. He speaks Spanish and English with equal fluency—yet he could not understand the Pachucos, who performed the neat trick of combining part of an English word with part of a Spanish word in building their own language.

Moreno said the Pachuco gangs developed from street gangs that had been operating in towns of the Southwest before, and the movement began to take shape—including the ducktail hair, the tatoo, the clothes—in El Paso. "Then for some reason Pachucos began going west from there," he said. "They flooded into the San Diego area during World War II. When those crew-cut Anglo servicemen spotted a ducktail Pachuco . . . well, you can guess what happened. The Pachuco War."

Even the origin of the word *Pachuco* is unclear. So is the origin of *Chicano*. Moreno thinks Pachuco was first used by a Mexican comedian who used the stage name Tin Tan. And, Moreno says, the word may have come from the Spanish *machucar*, which means to smash or crush. Generally accepted theory about *Chicano* is that it is contraction of *chico Mexicano*, little Mexican. The theory seems pretty slim if you bear in mind that a Spanish-speaking person would say *Mexicano chico*, not *chico Mexicano*. In Spanish, an inflective language, the modifier comes after the word it modifies, as in Rio Grande.

But back to the Pachucos. They rounded off their costume with a flat-top hat, flamenco-dancer style, and, in contrast to the hippie, slicked the black hair down, winding up with the hated (by Anglos) ducktail on the back of the neck.

Again unlike the hippie, the Pachuco was no flower child—
he was a hate child. And there I sat, cringing inwardly as I felt
that hate in the steady stare of the black eyes of Pablo. It was
something entirely new to me for several reasons. First, most
Pachucos were too old to be affected by the compulsory school
attendance law, which set the maximum, at that time, at fourteen. Since then it has been raised to sixteen. In the second place,
before that date, 1949, the system of distributing state money to
schools in Texas operated in such way as to discourage attendance
of Mexican-American children. And, of course, blacks.

Until the Gilmer-Aiken Law of 1949, funds were distributed
on the basis of the school census. Gilmer-Aiken changed it to
average daily attendance, referred to by school people as ADA.
To school administrators ADA has about the same meaning that
Dow-Jones does to stock brokers. In the past the Anglo-dominated
school systems, even in communities where the percentage of
Mexican-Americans was as high as 85, preferred that the Mexican-American children stay away from school—which they did
by the hundreds of thousands. It meant more money to spend on
Anglo children. After Gilmer-Aiken the school people began
beating the bushes to drag the Chicano kids to school. So that's
why I was facing the Pachuco with the switchblade.

Juanita was absent from school. That affected the ADA. Go
get her and bring her back to school. I went. I drove to the little
frame house in the eastern part of Austin, the city in which I
started my school social work career. I slushed through mud in
the street and across what would have been a sidewalk if one had
been put down. And slushed through mud in the yard.

The front door was slightly open, and I noticed two pairs of
shoes just outside the door. One women's, one for men. The men's
shoes weren't like any I had seen—high tops, thin, pointed toes.
Another part of the Pachuco costume—but I had forgotten all
the details.

Nobody answered my knock, and I called out, "Juanita, I know

you're in there. May I come in?" There was no answer. I sloshed
through mud to a nearby home where there was a telephone and
called the probation officer. "Can you come out and go in with
me?" I asked. "There is obviously a man in there with the girl."

"We can't go in without permission," he said. "It would be
breaking and entering."

That was quite a few years ago—before "No Knock" procedures were being suggested.

"The door is partly open," I said.

"Even if it's wide open, we still can't go in unless somebody
asks us or gives us permission."

"Well, could you phone Juanita's mother and bring her here
with you?"

"I'll do better than that," he said. "I'll go get her. But whoever
is in that house will probably be gone before we get there. Could
you sort of stand guard?"

"I'll try."

I stood guard by sitting in my car, watching. Today I would
stay in that car, no matter who went out the rear door. But I was
new at the work then and knew little about certain precautionary
techniques. So when I noticed that the shoes had been moved
inside, I decided the two were getting ready to leave by the back
door. I hurried to the front door. "Juanita, those shoes have been
moved, and I know you're in there," I said. "May I come in?"

After a pause I heard footsteps. Juanita opened the door and
said I could come in. After I entered the room, Pablo, wearing no
shirt, came in from the bedroom.

The ordeal finally ended. The probation officer and the
mother arrived, and the latter promptly began giving Juanita a
rough time. "Don't you know you're supposed to be in school?"
the mother said. "I don't know what I'm going to do with you.
You should be ashamed . . ." And so on.

"I can tell you what we'll do with him," the probation officer said, nodding toward Pablo. "We'll ship him right back to the reform school where he belongs. Contributing to the delinquency of a minor is all we need. And you might as well hand me that switchblade unless you want still more trouble."

Pablo had folded the switchblade and put it in his pocket. He took it out and handed it to the probation officer, who watched carefully as the transfer was made. A switchblade can be a deadly weapon when used by an expert. "We could send you back for this alone," the probation officer said, once the knife was safely in his hand.

The probation officer was right from a legal point of view. Being in a bedroom with a fourteen-year-old girl was sufficient reason for revoking parole. But Pablo was not sent back to reform school and Juanita did not go back to school. An examination by a doctor revealed that the girl was pregnant. At that time no pregnant girl, regardless of age, could continue attending classes in a public school.

Juvenile probation judges do not have the authority to force a young couple to marry. But the probation judge does have authority to revoke parole if certain conditions are not met. The condition he set: That Pablo get a job and marry Juanita. If not ... back to reform school.

Pablo got a job. He and Juanita were married. She was "permitted to withdraw" from school. I'm not exactly certain what the laws or regulations were in those days, but I do know that there were no married girls in junior high or high school at that time—and definitely no pregnant girls after the pregnancy became obvious.

So I closed my file on Juanita.

That was my first and last experience with a Pachuco, although I did, soon after that, make a visit to the state reform school, where I saw quite a few Pachucos. I couldn't recognize them by the costume or the haircut—or the switchblade, thank heavens. But the tatoo marks were there, so I knew.

But I have had quite a bit of experience with Chicanos, for they began to figure prominently in school affairs in many South Texas cities by the time I took leave in 1970. I had no trouble with any of them—well, let's say I had no trouble with them just because they called themselves Chicanos and became activists. They were struggling, within the framework of the law, for equality . . . for a voice in the affairs of *their* nation. Why should I have trouble with them?

Rotating Baby-sitters

The first time I went to the home of Mrs. Rosa Cantu I barely avoided being run down by a wheelchair. Too bad. It might have made me famous. At least, I've never heard of anyone being run down by a wheelchair, so my case would have been a first.

Mrs. Cantu, a wide grin on her face, was in the chair. Propelled by four boys, all shouting and scrambling for places to hold, the chair came zipping at me, and I jumped back just in time to avoid being hit. I shouted to the crippled woman and the boys, but none heard me as they reached the street and moved into high gear.

"Where are they going?" I asked a little girl standing in front of a nearby home.

"Rummage sale," she said. "This is the day of the big rummage sale, and Mrs. Cantu loves it."

I drove away, planning to return the following day. I wanted to talk to Mrs. Cantu about an astonishingly clever trick she was playing on the school system. And as I talked to her, the following day, I realized why she had been able to carry on a sort of rotating baby-sitter system that the school people never suspected. She could do it because she was a remarkable woman in many ways.

She had four children—a boy in high school, a girl in junior high school, a girl in elementary school, and a two-year-old boy at home.

I had become suspicious when I checked absentee records in the three schools and noticed a difinite pattern being followed by the Cantu children. I did not work at the high school level, but I called the school and checked the attendance record of the boy. There definitely was a pattern. This woman, doomed to live out her life in a wheelchair, was rotating her children, keeping one at home every day to act as baby-sitter—for her as well as for the two-year-old. She had to have help. She was so badly crippled by arthritis that she couldn't even move onto and off the commode without help. Yet she was shrewd enough to rotate the children as baby-sitters in such way that the school people failed to notice.

Absenteeism is so common among poor Mexican-American children—and Mrs. Cantu was on relief—that school people accept it as inevitable. Especially if the child never misses more than three days in succession. In that case, I am called in and asked to go to the home and check the situation. No Cantu child was absent three days in a row, so I was not called in. But I finally detected that rotating pattern, quite by accident, and began probing. And came near to getting run down by a wheelchair right at the beginning of my probe.

Mrs. Cantu smiled pleasantly and asked me to sit down. I

noticed the hands, so twisted that she could not handle a telephone. She had tried because the Welfare people insisted. The two-year-old boy suffered from epileptic seizures, so Welfare said Mrs. Cantu must have a telephone, for which they paid, in case of emergency. The telephone was installed, but Mrs. Cantu could not use it. She solved that problem, just as she seemed to solve all others. One of the children—the baby-sitter on that particular day—would hold the telephone to Mrs. Cantu's ear as she talked. But, independent soul that she was, that solution wasn't quite enough. She wanted a telephone with a gadget on it so she could rest it on her shoulder and cradle it against her ear. Then nobody would have to hold it for her. If she ever got the cradle telephone, I never saw it.

"Chelo is here at home when she should be at school," I said, a seemingly unnecessary remark, since Chelo was sitting beside us, listening.

"I must have someone to help me," the mother said. She frankly admitted the rotating baby-sitter system but said it would end the following week. "My sister is moving in Sunday," she said. "She has seven children."

"Seven children! And you have four. You mean eleven children and two grown people are going to live in this small house?"

"Just for a little while," she said.

I knew Welfare would blow its lid. But that was Welfare's problem. I stuck to my job, which was to keep the children in school—and to help them in school if they needed help.

"When my sister comes, there will be children who don't go to school but are old enough to help me," Mrs. Cantu said.

"What about your sister's husband?"

"He ran off and left her the way my husband did me when I got sick. My husband was gone four years. Then he came back."

"And left again?"

"He stayed long enough to give me the little one there," and she nodded toward the baby on the floor.

In Texas the child-support law is mostly a lot of printing in neat legal terminology. Having the father jailed, which is done occasionally, seems to accomplish nothing. It can make matters worse, since a man in jail makes no money. One judge once adopted the ingenious scheme of ordering the father to spend weekends in jail, but he let the father out during the week to earn child-support money. Another judge set aside every Wednesday to listen to child-support arguments. "You come visit some Wednesday," he said. "We call it Father's Day around here." Texans wouldn't tolerate for a second the child-support laws enforced in California. Texas is still legally a *man's* state.

"I think you are doing fine," I told the mother. "I'll come back and see you again next week."

Sure enough, all three Cantu children were in school all week. But Welfare objected, as I had expected, when people with the organization learned that two adults and eleven children were living in one four-room house. The sister, also on welfare, finally arranged to rent a house next door. She took her brood with her, and everything seemed in order, since two of her preschool children did the baby-sitting for Mrs. Cantu.

Now and then I would see Mrs. Cantu being whisked along some street at an alarming clip, three or four boys furnishing the horsepower for her wheelchair. She had two wheelchairs, a conventional one to use in the home and an ordinary armchair equipped with rollers that she used for traveling. The boys pushed her to the clinic for treatments, to rummage sales, which were her major delight in life, to church, which she enjoyed but the boys didn't, and to the grocery store. The woman had a will of iron. Such people are rare.

Then bingo! The sister ran off with a man, leaving her seven children with no one to care for them except the crippled Mrs. Cantu. There was nothing to do, in Mrs. Cantu's opinion, but take them in and care for them. So the whole covey, eleven strong, was back with her. Once more Welfare boiled over. Mrs. Cantu could *not* have eleven children in her little home, especially since seven of them were not hers and she was crippled and had an epileptic child . . . and . . .

"All right, you do something," she told Welfare.

They couldn't think of much to do except furnish a housekeeper to work three days a week at the Cantu home. The housekeeper spent much of her time washing clothes, the rest cleaning house, cooking, and helping Mrs. Cantu with the epileptic child.

A few months later the baby had a severe seizure, and school administrators permitted the older girl to stay with the child at the hospital. The stay was long, but the doctor was hopeful that the seizures were under control, since a new medicine was being used and it seemed to be effective. The doctor was right. I never heard of another seizure, and I visited Mrs. Cantu at fairly frequent intervals during a period of three years. She was one of my regulars. If I had no specific reason to go, I might drop by just for a social visit. This woman fascinated me. She made all the rest of us seem weak and petty with our complaints.

The runaway sister was abandoned by her boyfriend and returned to the children, taking her brood of seven back into the little house next door. But the sister didn't stay. Men seemed much more entertaining than the children, so it was back to the Cantu home for the brood—eleven children again. I never knew whether I would find four or eleven children at the home. Neither did Mrs. Cantu, since her sister was rotating men about as regularly as Mrs. Cantu had been rotating baby-sitters. And Welfare never knew, a situation that caused infinite trouble for the agency. They would send a housekeeper, then withdraw the housekeeper. All properly confusing. But . . . over the long haul, that crippled, abandoned woman did a far better job with her children than many middle-income parents do with theirs.

We let Carlos, the oldest, drop out of school when he was sixteen. He had got a job, and it was evident that he was not going to do more in school, even if we forced him to attend. And forcing him was pretty doubtful. He was interested in his job, not in school.

Adelia, the older girl, wasn't doing very well at school, due partly to absenteeism. The time she had spent at the hospital with the sick child and all those days of baby-sitting before I moved in combined with other factors to hold her back. "How would you like to be my office helper?" I asked her during one of our conferences.

"I would love it," she said. "Last year they let me help in the library one day a week and I liked that."

"All right, you will be my office helper," I said. "Report tomorrow. I will arrange it with the principal."

Adelia failed to show at the appointed time. I saw her the following day and asked why.

"You can't be an office helper unless you make a B average," she said sadly. "They announced on the loud speaker yesterday not to apply unless you had a B average." Adelia had an average grade of C. She could have done better . . . she was a bright girl. "I wanted so much to be your office helper," she said, on the verge of tears.

Here was another entirely unnecessary gap in the child-adult relationship—one that could be closed and should be closed when circumstances indicate such procedure. A young person wants to be a part of life. He *wants* responsibility, *wants* to work, especially if it seems that the work might lead to a better life. But . . . a C average is an insurmountable barrier. I have not kept records, but I have seen similar situations hundreds of times. Occasionally I can break the barrier—arrange for the child to work in the cafeteria, help in the library, be a messenger. We don't give the young enough chance to participate . . . then we wonder why and how and when we lost contact. Such participation can be quite valuable to a child unless he considers it a form of punishment. Some principals take that attitude, and the results are unfortunate.

"You *will* be my office helper," I assured Adelia. "Don't worry about it at all. Come with me and we will get a special exception from the principal."

And we did, mainly because the principal was a reasonable man and he and I had worked out a harmonious relationship in dealing with children referred to me. Suddenly Adelia became a *person*—my office helper. And from then on her school work was satisfactory.

The last time I saw her she told me, her face beaming, that she was making good enough grades to go to high school and that she *was* going to high school. "I am going to be a secretary," she said.

"Like you were my office helper?" I asked.

"A regular secretary in an office. I'll do it some day, when I get more education."

The younger girl, called Sammy for reasons I could not find out ("They just call me Sammy," she said), was eleven and in the fourth grade, one year behind. But she began doing better after the rotating baby-sitter business ended.

Along toward the shank end of my three years' relationship with Mrs. Cantu, the sister was back home, apparently for good, and Mrs. Cantu was relieved of the burden of the seven children. All very fine. Or was it? All but one of the sister's children were now of school age. And, reluctant as I was to face the facts, I checked and learned that Mrs. Cantu was now rotating her sister's children—school-age ones—as baby-sitters. She wasn't going to pass up that pleasure, especially considering all the months and years she had cared for those children.

Of course I never considered filing charges against Mrs. Cantu when she kept some of her younger nieces out of school to baby-sit—and I knew that she did that occasionally. Who wants to drag a wheelchair woman—a cripple on relief—into court and try to get her jailed for violating the compulsory school law? I certainly wasn't going to. But the sister—ah, that was different. And the sister was on welfare. Let her baby-sit for Mrs. Cantu, but send the kids to school.

The situation never came to a head, for I decided to take a leave at the end of the 1969–70 school year. And it looks as though the leave may last a long time. As for Mrs. Cantu—away she goes, zipping along in her wheelchair, headed for the rummage sale. And she has been and is a good mother—the kind of mother who might set an example.

I don't try to understand all the complex angles of such human relationships, and I am not inclined to toss out pat answers. But one thing might be carefully considered: There was shared responsibility in that home—mutual interest in common goals, limited as those goals were. There was dependence and there was interdependence. All were permitted to participate—were expected to participate. All did. All had a sense of being needed.

I Signed My Character Away

"Ladies and gentlemen, in this corner we have Mrs. Helen Bond, age 62, weight 147 pounds. She is armed with an ice pick. And in this corner we have her daughter-in-law, Mrs. Lulu Johnson, age 43, weight 138 pounds. She is armed with a pair of sharp scissors. Come out fighting, and may the best lady win."

That speech might well have served as an introduction to the long, savage feud between these two women over possession of Mrs. Johnson's husband and children. There were matches and rematches. On occasion pistols flashed, although no shots were fired—at least none that I was informed about.

"When I was coming out of my place of work, she jumped me with an ice pick," Mrs. Johnson told me. The place where she worked was a beer tavern. "She was ready to kill me if she had to before she would let me marry her son. I just happened to have a pair of sharp-pointed scissors in my purse. I got them out and I knew exactly what I was going to do with them. I was going to clamp down on the handles to close the points. Then I was going to work them around inside, and, if I had, I'd of killed her for sure. But her husband got ahold of us and pulled me off her."

She convinced me that the wild stories I had heard about people from the Big Thicket were true. At least some of them. "You've had trouble with your mother-in-law since then?" I asked.

"Nothing but battling her for twenty-five years," Mrs. Johnson said. "Once I signed my character away to be sure she didn't get my kids."

I didn't understand her comment but decided not to interrupt her story.

"She made a mess with her own kids," Mrs. Johnson continued. "That's why my husband is in the penitentiary today. Then she wanted to get his children, my kids, and ruin them. So I signed my character away to keep her from getting them. But she's still after the young ones . . ."

This was my first contact with any people of the Big Thicket, the vast, swampy forest that blankets a large part of East Texas.

I went to Mrs. Johnson's home because the school psychologist found that her youngest boy, Willie, was mentally retarded. He had an IQ of 58, barely high enough to get in school at that time. He was classified as educable. Those with IQs below 50 were not considered educable, and few schools except those in some of the larger cities of Texas would take them. In the cities special classes were usually available for such children, most of whom were considered trainable even if they were not educable. That is, they could be taught to feed themselves and go to the toilet and bathe and dress and perhaps do a few simple household chores. Maybe learn some simple craft later.

The school people wanted to put Willie in a special education class for the mentally retarded. We needed the mother's consent, so I visited her and explained.

"Sure, I think his mind is a little weak," she said. "Just like his Daddy. You know, his Daddy hit him over the head when he was little and he fell back against some boards. There was some nails in the boards. I think that made his mind a little weak."

Mrs. Johnson was probably wrong about brain damage. Tests showed that Willie was mentally retarded, but there was no evidence of organic damage. You can blame genes for mental retardation; a physical injury, such as insufficient oxygen, for brain injury or brain damage. Of course the brain injury may be so severe that the child, or adult, is also mentally retarded. It is not necessarily that way. Many cases of MBI (minimal brain injury) that we encounter have close to the average-range IQ—some an astonishing 140. By general definition, the mentally retarded have an IQ below 70. Obviously, lumping the two together in the same class and giving them the same training and teaching is not a sound procedure. But it has been done in many schools.

But why should I try to explain to Mrs. Johnson? If I undertook to convince her that Willie's trouble was genetic—it was only one more step to deciding which side of the family was to "blame," and there was enough friction in this family already.

Mrs. Johnson broke off the discussion about Willie and launched a tirade against her mother-in-law. It was sensational, explosive. Big Thicket fire. The Men of the Thicket, as these Anglo descendants of pioneer Texans are called, are a breed apart, a few of them still clinging stubbornly to a way of life that no longer fits into the general pattern. They resemble the descendants of the cedar choppers in the Texas hill country, who also clung to a way of life long after the rest of Texas changed.

Some of the Men of the Thicket are mean, which you would expect, since they have made their living, such as it is, by operating outside the law. At first they were fire hunters—they hunted deer at night by the light of old carbide headlights and sold the meat. That went out of style when the deer population dwindled and when a few fire hunters were killed by ranchers and game wardens, and others locked in prison for several years. Then it was making white lightning, bootleg booze. When the Prohibition era faded, many of the Men of the Thicket turned to telephoning catfish. No, you can not carry on a conversation with a catfish by telephone. But you can, by vigorously cranking an old-style telephone, from which two wires dangle down in the water, cause a catfish to become paralyzed and rise to the surface, belly up. The catfish answered the ring . . . and Men of the Thicket continued making a living outside the law.

People of the whole country got a vague idea, outrageously exaggerated, of Men of the Thicket when Roy Harris of Cut and Shoot was matched, or mismatched, with Floyd Patterson for the heavyweight boxing title. Press and radio and TV people made much of the little community called Cut and Shoot. The name did not derive from wholesale cutting and shooting. It had a truly prosaic origin—came from cutting chute, the name of a contraption used to load cattle into box cars. Thicket people pronounced it "Cut'n Chute," and eventually it became, to the general public, "Cut and Shoot." The press never bothered to check on this. Why do so? As J. Frank Dobie once wrote, why let facts intrude upon the validity of the imagination?

Well, Mrs. Johnson was from Cut and Shoot. So was her husband. So was her mother-in-law. They had moved to the northern part of Houston and settled in a community with other poor Anglos, mostly from the Thicket and the Piney Woods. They retained their pride—and their inclination to switch quickly from violent words to violent actions. Before I got through with the Johnson clan, I decided that the newspaper and radio and TV people were right. The proper name for the place is Cut and Shoot, not Cutting Chute.

"Yes ma'am, I signed my character away," Mrs. Johnson repeated. "That's when I put the older ones in the Star of Hope Home."

There were seven Johnson children. The two oldest boys were in military service when I was called in on the case. The oldest girl was married. That left four, and the mother-in-law, after twenty years of battling, was still trying to get custody of them.

"And what made things worse was that my own mother was trying to get them kids away from me," Mrs. Johnson went on. "When I think of the things she throwed at me, calling me a two-bit whore—excuse me—and saying I rolled men and all that stuff."

"Your own mother?"

"My own mother." She bit out the words. "You remember back in the WPA days . . . I was on WPA and they gave us orange stamps and green stamps but that was just for groceries. Couldn't buy no cigarettes with them. So my mother said to me, 'I want some tobacco. Why don't you go out and get some money? Why don't you get hold of some man and get some money for tobacco?' And I told her she was a woman, and if one of us was going out whoring to get tobacco money, she could do it. It didn't do no good. She called the law and had them come out, saying my kids didn't have enough food to eat, and that's what went against me strong. Now I want you to know that I keep chicken and pork and fresh liver in that ice box all the time. Nobody's coming out here and say I don't have fresh food for my kids."

Mrs. Johnson had learned to battle. And she had to do it alone, since Wilbur, her husband, was serving his fifth term in the penitentiary.

"The woman at the Star of Hope Home told me that the best

way for the Home to get custody of my three oldest children was to sign how I'd been laying up with different men—unfit mother, I think she called it. I told her that if I had to sign my character away to keep Mama or that bitch—excuse me—of a mother-in-law from getting them kids, I'd do it. And I did."

"I understand now," I said, smiling in an effort to convince her that I was on her side. The smile was a mistake, for she immediately remembered her obligations as a hostess and said, "Let me get you some coffee."

"I'd like it," I said, even though I had seen a roach and some other bugs moving about the place. When she started wiping spots—bug spots, I presumed—off the inside of the coffee cups I felt a trifle weak. But you don't shy away from bug spots if there's a chance to help a woman regain a sense of self-respect.

"Yes, I signed papers saying I was running around with men," Mrs. Johnson continued. "But she never quit, that mother-in-law. She sued me and the Star of Hope Home trying to get the three children, and her lawyer brought up about me living with her son four years before we got married. Sure, we did because she wouldn't turn him loose. I finally faced up to the old bitch—excuse me. I was the only one with the guts to do it. Her son doggone sure wouldn't. He's weak—weak in the head like little Willie. Anyway, that woman went into court again. Trying to get the young'uns away from me and the judge said to me, 'Mrs. Johnson, are you married now?' I said, 'Judge, if I ain't married now they better give me back my five dollars at the courthouse cause there's where I got this piece of paper.' I didn't tell him my husband was in the penitentiary. I didn't have to—he knew. I laid that marriage paper on the bench and the judge said I was married at that time and that's all he needed to know, not what happened in the past."

She paused, and there was no escape—I had to sip coffee from the bug-spotted cup.

"That woman, my mother-in-law, and her lawyer took the case all the way up to the top court," Mrs. Johnson continued. "But she lost. And after that the judge said I could have full custody of all my children. But the three older ones was getting along fine at the Star of Hope Home, so I let them stay a little longer. Then the boys went into the service and the girl got married. But nobody can do anything for Wilbur . . . that's my husband. He's still Mama's little boy. So he goes out and steals and gets back in the penitentiary and I'm here by myself to fight for my kids. I'll fight for them."

I didn't doubt that—and probably a lot more effectively than Roy Harris fought Floyd Patterson.

"And that husband . . . the last time they sent him up I figured I'd had enough. I went and got me a divorce. Let Mama have him, but she'll have to go to the pen to baby him. Maybe she'd have been different if somebody else had faced up to her the way I did—and years before. But nobody would. She's got a daughter that's scared to death of her . . . forty-four-year-old woman that's afraid to marry because Mama might not like it."

I told Mrs. Johnson I would return in two weeks and give her a report on Willie.

She had a lot to tell me on my next visit and still more during subsequent visits, which I made because the two boys who were older than Willie were terrifying teachers and children at the school. The boys were new at the school—family had moved into our district only a short time before. It seemed that still more of her brood might be headed for Star of Hope Home—or the state reform school. Maybe they would have blended into the general pattern at Cut and Shoot. They sure didn't at Allen elementary.

"I called that principal at Overton school," Mrs. Johnson said. That was the school from which Willie was transferred when the family moved into our district. "They kept poor little

Willie in first grade about three or four times and called him
a liar and a thief and they never went to the trouble to find out
he was weak in the mind. Well, I sure told off that principal."
Thicket people in action. "I told her 'This is Mrs. Johnson, Willie's mother. You led that little Willie a dog's life in that school.
I want you to know in the Allen school where he is now they
examined the little fellow and found out he is retarded . . .' " She
had trouble with the word *retarded* but managed it.

"The principal sure sounded surprised and kept saying, 'why
we didn't know he was mentally retarded, we just thought he
wouldn't mind anybody and wouldn't study and caused trouble!'
I told her, 'Well, the next time you get a little boy like that in
your school, before you start calling him a liar and a thief you
might find out if something is wrong with his mind.' I told her
plenty of other things, but . . ." She hesitated—I wondered about
those "other things."

"Maybe you helped some other little children by telling her
that," I said. She seemed very pleased. "We think Willie will
do a lot better, now that he is in a class where the teacher is
trained to help children like him," I said.

"Are there many others like little Willie?" she asked.

"Quite a few. Enough to have special classes for them."

"Well, I'm right pleased to know they're helping him." Then
she became despondent. She had lost her job.

According to the rules of the "Poverty Game," Mrs. Johnson
was required to inform Welfare if she earned any money by
working. Whatever she earned would be deducted from relief
money. She was getting the relief money on the theory that she
was staying home, taking care of the young children. I had heard
that she was working again, in a tavern, about the only job she
seemed able to handle. But I said nothing about it. Let Welfare
do its own investigating. And I'm quite sure Mrs. Johnson never
reported her income from work.

"My boss got drunk last night and cussed everybody in the place," she said. "He's a mighty fine man when he's sober, but he gets mean when he's drunk. When I couldn't get them tickets for the customers wrote out fast enough, he cussed me out. He'll be sorry when he sobers up."

How many thousands of times I have listened to that observation, "He's the finest fellow in the world when he's sober."

"I wanted to buy better clothes for my children," Mrs. Johnson said, as though explaining why she was working—and without letting Welfare know. "I don't want people looking out and saying, 'There goes one of them sorry, lowdown Johnson kids.' "

Pride. It can be a sustaining force in life. Or, if it is unrealistic, it can be a destructive force.

Four months later, shortly before the end of the school year, Mrs. Johnson came breezing into my office wearing a new dress and looking like a different person. She was beaming. "I want you to meet Mr. Wilcox, my husband," she said with pride. He was a tall, rugged-looking man of about forty-five, and he wore trim ranch clothes. As we talked briefly I got the impression that he was brighter than average, easygoing . . . the kind of man many a woman in her mid-forties would be happy to get.

"I wanted John—that's my husband—to meet you because you've done so much for me and my children," Mrs. Johnson said.

"I'm hoping the boys'll kind of like life out at the ranch," Wilcox said.

"John's ranch is at Cut and Shoot," Mrs. Johnson said. "His wife died a couple of years ago and his children are gone . . . he got tired of being lonesome."

"Those boys may teach him the blessings of loneliness," I was thinking. I still couldn't quite figure it out. This woman, in her mid-forties, burdened with one mentally retarded boy and two wild ones . . . this fiery battler getting a quiet, evidently desirable husband . . . a man with a ranch.

There is small reward in guessing who will marry whom, and even less reward in reasoning why. Maybe John Wilcox looked forward to having two boys that he could brag about in Cut and Shoot—"I'll bet my boys is tougher'n yours." I doubted that. But on one point there was no room for doubt. The two boys just above Willie in age suddenly, almost miraculously, quieted down and became practically models of behavior. The teachers marveled but were alert, expecting a trick.

I got the answer from Andrew, the older of the two boys. "Our new daddy says we can ride horses on the ranch and hunt squirrels and catch fish and camp out on the creek and all kinds of things like that if we are good boys in school," Andrew said.

A ranch of their own! And back home—back to Cut and Shoot. So everybody—teachers, principals, boys, parents, and I were happy when the whole Johnson clan piled into John Wilcox's truck at the end of school and headed for Cut and Shoot. I expected no miracles—I had abandoned such dreamy hopes years before. But maybe at Cut and Shoot the boys would fit better into the general pattern—maybe meet boys tougher than they. And for entertainment they could telephone catfish instead of rifling the lockers of other children. At any rate, they were gone. I wish them the good life.

The Louse War

I drove to the home of Hilda Galvan knowing that this wasn't the kind of visit I was going to enjoy. If educators generally had a clear idea of all the things that happen when a school social worker visits homes of problem children, the euphemistic term "visiting teacher" would no longer be used in referring to social workers. They were called visiting teachers in earlier days because the word "social" raised eyebrows in Texas.

I had been to the Galvan home before, checking on truancy and vandalism by the older boys in the family. I knew just what kind of fireball Mrs. Galvan was.

Now it was Hilda, age twelve and blessed, in the opinion of Mrs. Galvan and her *curandera*, with nits in the hair. Victor

Krause, the principal, had sent Hilda home, instructing her not to return until her hair was free of nits. When the child failed to return in the allotted span—three days—I was called in. Routine procedure, although there certainly wasn't anything routine about the case.

I proceeded as diplomatically as I could. My diplomacy back-fired . . . seemed to stoke up the mother's fiery reaction. "Hilda hasn't been to school in three days," I said.

"And you know why?" the mother shot back. "That principal kicked her out."

Hilda sat on the sofa, obviously embarrassed. The nits in her long, straight black hair were clearly visible.

"Well, the case was referred to me by the principal," I said. "We have certain rules . . ."

"You have rules for Mexican children," the mother cut in. "Do you send the blonde girls home?"

"If we see nits we do," I said. "But it isn't easy to see nits in light blond hair, especially if it's curly."

"Especially if you don't look close," the mother added. "Anyway, Hilda doesn't have nits. That's dandruff."

I didn't argue with her. I had tried that when we were having trouble with one of her older children, a boy.

"And if she had nits," the mother continued, "that would be a sign that she is healthy. The *curandera* says so."

Again I didn't argue. I had heard over and over that the *curanderos* and *curanderas* (women) stated firmly that the presence of head lice or nits, or both, proved good health. It was hailed as a good sign when an infant baby had nits in its hair. At least the presence of active head lice proves that the child is alive—lice take off instantly when a person dies. And the *curanderos* say they leave if a child is sick—has a fever.

If you think the institution of the *curandero* has vanished in the vast Great Barrio area from the Gulf of Mexico to the Pacific, go talk to some of the poorer, uneducated Mexican-Americans in that area. Most of those people have been denied the services of medical doctors. They couldn't pay; therefore, no doctor. The *curandero* was as firmly entrenched in their life pattern as Mother Church—the Catholic church. The *curandero* is a combination medical doctor (if you admit that administering extracts from herbs is doctoring) and faith healer. I have watched as a *curandero* moved a wand over a sick child, from head to foot and back again, mumbling in an unknown tongue. Well, it sounded that way to me. I don't know Spanish, but I know how it sounds. Texas authorities have waged occasional battles against *curanderos*, with no long-range results. And Mrs. Galvan put her faith in a *curandera*, woman faith-herb doctor.

It is interesting to note that that the word *curandero* comes from the word *curar*, which means to cure, and that poor people in Mexico and parts of Texas call the village priest *cura*—the healer. The *curandero* is the lay healer.

Anyway, Mrs. Galvan's *curandera* had assured her that lice in the hair meant good health, which was a little puzzling, since Mrs. Galvan had finished high school, spoke English with very little accent, and was brighter than the average, including Anglos. In most cases a high school graduate loses faith in the *curandero*. Not Mrs. Galvan, who kept insisting that I talk to her *curandera*.

I told her I would report back to the principal. Let Krause fight his Louse War, as it came to be called in the school system.

Krause began boiling over much in the manner that Mrs. Galvan did. "I guess she wants to spread lice all over the school, so all the children will be *healthy*," he said. "Such stupid nonsense."

"I doubt if you are going to change her beliefs," I warned. "You might as well try to pull her away from Mother Church."

Krause never heeded warnings. Another bulldozer. "I'm going

to stop this spreading of lice in our school," he said. "Let's go back there—I'll show that mother that those white spots aren't dandruff."

"There might be fireworks," I again warned.

"I'll take care of that."

Krause was a rigid disciplinarian, and to him the prime virtues in life were those prized by his Germanic ancestors who came to Texas around the middle of the past century, many settling in the area near San Antonio. The virtues are, of course, cleanliness, thrift, and hard work. That's okay with me. I'm strongly in favor of such virtues, but I seldom try to force them on others.

Krause had launched the Louse War single-handed, but he was able to recruit followers in a short time. Two other principals were now enforcing his no-louse policy—sending home any child who had head lice or nits. I saw some of the results now and then as I drove to various homes in the district. Children playing on the streets during school hours. I would stop and talk to them. They said they had been kicked out because they had nits, and usually I could see the nits. Krause and the two other principals were getting rid of school kids, not nits.

As the principal and I approached Mrs. Galvan's home, I considered warning him once more. But, as I didn't think he had even heard my previous warning, I decided to let him find out the hard way. He did.

Mrs. Galvan was a panther. I had watched another principal turn pale as she ripped him apart in a truancy case. We had scarcely entered Mrs. Galvan's home until Krause blurted out, "Hilda has lice. We can't put up with that at school."

"She does *not* have lice!" Mrs. Galvan exploded. "Let's see you find one."

Krause had made two mistakes in two sentences, one factual, the other procedural. "Well, she has nits," he hedged, trying to remedy one mistake. "And they hatch out into lice. I can see the nits from here."

"That's dandruff," the mother said.

"They're nits and I can prove it," Krause said. Push on, the big fool said, push on. "We're getting complaints from parents that their children are catching lice at school. People consider them a sign of filth . . ." Mistake No. 3.

"You talk about filth," Mrs. Galvan shouted, her black eyes blazing. "I saw you spit on my porch. What could be filthier than spitting on a person's floor? Do you spit on the floor in your home, or do you save your spit for Mexicans?"

There was a catch in Krause's breath, and for the first time since I had been around him he was, momentarily, at a loss for words. But he started again . . . push on. "I'll prove they are nits," he said, lifting a strand of Hilda's hair that had white specks on it. He tapped the strand of hair sharply with a pencil. The specks held firm—dandruff would have fallen off. "See. I told you!" the principal said triumphantly. "They *are* nits."

The mother said nothing for a moment, but I could see the tornado cloud building.

"You'll have to get those nits out of her hair before she can come back to school," Krause said.

The tornado hit. "You take her back or you'll be sorry," Mrs. Galvan said. "I'll get a lawyer and drag you into court and make you take her back." She moved nearer, shouting right in Krause's face. "It's one of your cheap tricks to get rid of Mexican children," she told him. "Maybe blond Anglo children take lice to school, but the Mexicans always get the blame. They're filthy . . . and you . . . you spit on my floor."

Krause was backing away, hunting for words. Mrs. Galvan was pursuing him, unloading words. "You . . . you and the rest of your Germans have beat us down for years because we are Mexicans," she snapped. "I know. I went to that school. I was treated like an animal."

She made the reference to Germans because not too long ago the Germanic minority in the community did hold most of the positions on the school board. Then those of German ancestry joined the Anglo Baptists and continued in control, even though the district is 70 percent Mexican-American. Later the Mexican-Americans took over. It didn't last.

Finally Mrs. Galvan said, "I've got to go to work now. But if you don't have Hilda back in school today, I'll see you tomorrow with my lawyer." She swished angrily out of the home.

"Nobody can talk to me like that," Krause said.

"She just did," I reminded him.

"Well, Hilda, I'm not going to take you back until you get those nits out," he told the child. She said nothing—the kind of response Krause was accustomed to when he issued an order. "Do you understand?" he persisted. The girl merely nodded, looking at him with cold hatred.

As we were driving back to school I reminded Krause that a similar situation in another school had resulted in court action that evidently had set a precedent. "We had a girl, a blonde girl of German ancestry, I believe," I told him. "That was several years ago in another school. She had nits in her hair and the principal wouldn't let her go to school. The girl's parents went to a doctor, who certified that the girl was not suffering from a contagious disease and could not be kept out of school on account of the nits. That mother will go into court, just as she said. She's a battler. Chances are she will win, and we won't look so good."

"I am *not* going to have lice in my school," Krause repeated.

Few of the poorer Mexican-Americans knew at that time what their rights were, and many of those who knew were reluctant to go into court and demand those rights. There has been change, a vast change, in this situation. There is now a legal rights agency prepared to handle cases in which Mexican-Americans and others are, or may be, deprived of their rights.

Crowding is a major factor in the spread of head lice. Color of the skin has nothing to do with it; lice are color blind—in fact, they don't even have eyes. Mexican-Americans make up the bulk of the unskilled labor force in South Texas and elsewhere in the Southwest. They live in poorer homes, where there is more crowding. And they usually have larger families, due to lack of birth control knowledge and the dictates of Mother Church. Two, three, even four children may sleep in one bed. And the head lice roam. So there are actually more cases of lice and nits in the head hair of Mexican-American children. And I doubt if filth is a factor, although it may be in the survival of body lice, about which I know nothing.

Head lice can be easily transferred by combs, both the old-style fine-tooth, generally used to remove lice, and ordinary combs. For this reason teachers and administrators are constantly warning girls not to borrow or lend combs. I say girls, because until recently boys cut their hair so short that lice didn't find it a welcome homesite. That began changing a short time before I left, and now I wonder if teachers are battling head lice in that long hair of so many schoolboys. And as I said, the louse has a staunch ally in the person of the *curandero*.

I let Krause cool off for a couple of days. Hilda was still out of school, but I sure wasn't going to file any truancy charges if I could avoid it. Then I talked the principal into letting the child return to school on condition that I work out an agreement with the mother. "Nits do not move from head to head," I reminded the principal.

"But they hatch . . ."

"If you let me handle this, I think I can work it out."

"How much time do you want?"

"About two weeks. And remember—if we go into court, or are dragged in there, that mother is going to make us look pretty sad. And she may not wait on us."

Krause agreed, but he still clung to his kickout policy in dealing with other children. He was setting a pattern of action that was certain to backfire. The two other principals who were following his kickout policy in the Louse War began getting worried. ADA (average daily attendance) was sagging . . . the Louse War was rapidly building to a climax. I figured this situation would work in my favor if I could stall things.

First I had to make peace with Mrs. Galvan, and I certainly felt uneasy when she opened the door and asked me in. There was no need for uneasiness. She greeted me cordially and said she wanted me to know that her remarks were for the benefit of the principal alone, not me.

"I think school policy in this situation is going to change soon," I told her, and I noticed Hilda, again sitting on the sofa listening, brighten up at once. She had a fairly high IQ, made good grades, and was determined to finish high school and then get some vocational training—about the highest goal most poor Mexican-American children dared set.

"I've talked to my lawyer," Mrs. Galvan said. "That principal had better get Hilda back in school."

"The principal is willing to let me take her back right now if you and Hilda will just promise to do a few things to help," I said.

"Do what things?"

"Shampoo Hilda's hair with one of those medicines." The school always sent out printed instructions for dealing with lice and nits. But the instructions were in English only, and the parents of many of the poorer Mexican-American children did not understand English. The school nurse recommended four medicines, including kerosene.

"If you shampoo her hair every day and get somebody to pick out the nits and keep them picked out, there won't be any more trouble," I said.

"I will shampoo her hair . . . even though she doesn't have nits." Mrs. Galvan wasn't going to abandon her guns. "And I'll see that she combs it twice a day, here at home. But I don't have the money right now to pay a nit picker."

See where the term "nit picker" came from? In the barrios nit picking is an honorable profession, and the nit picker is proud of her work—so proud that she will not take on a case unless she is guaranteed pay for five sessions. She might miss a few nits and her reputation would be ruined.

"It won't cost one-tenth as much as what you would have to pay your lawyer if you don't send Hilda back," I told her. "You see, things are different now. I am authorized to take Hilda back to school today."

The mother finally agreed to turn the case over to a professional nit picker she knew. She said she would start the course Saturday, when Robert, her oldest, got his pay.

Robert had been quite a headache to us when he was in junior high. He was my first contact with glue sniffing. Since I work mostly with elementary children, and some in intermediate schools, I have had little experience with marijuana, glue sniffing, and so on. I would undoubtedly get plenty of experience if I returned.

Robert not only sniffed glue, but he also was converting an entire group of youngsters to his way of life, staging parties at his home while his mother was at work. Finally, the junior high principal agreed to let him withdraw when he was sixteen and had a chance to work at a nearby military base. He had been doing fine on his job.

He came through in grand style in the Louse War. Even volunteered to get the whole house fumigated—by some of his pals at the military base—while his mother was at work.

A few days later the superintendent called the principals and social workers and nurses and counselors together for a policy statement in the Louse War. On the face of it, the kickout policy seemed unchanged by his new regulations, for the notice to parents read, "All lice and all eggs, both alive and dead, must be removed from the hair before your child will be allowed to return to school."

The big change was in the kickout days. All school lice inspections were scheduled for Friday. The child was "kicked out" after the last bell Friday afternoon and the parents were notified not to send the child back to school until Monday morning. Very neat. How can a child go to school during the weekend when all the buildings are closed? Thus ended the Louse War.

The Christmas Tree

The young mother, moderately attractive, neatly dressed, and thoroughly frightened, broke down under the strain and poured out to the psychiatrist the story of shame that she had tried to keep to herself.

You can talk freely to a psychiatrist, she had been told. There is a rigid code. Psychiatrists never pass on anything told them by patients. That's what she had been told. So out came the story that had been torturing her for years. Her six-year-old son Carl Ray was illegitimate. His natural father was in prison. His stepfather, one of the few other persons who knew the truth, hated the boy and beat him unmercifully—or completely ignored him.

The young mother lived in constant dread that her son would, because of mistreatment, follow the life pattern of his father.

And her fears appeared well founded, for at the tender age of six Carl Ray was an astonishingly proficient thief, a cheat, a liar, and a budding pyromaniac. One of the first things he did the following year, when the family moved and he entered second grade in one of my schools, was build up a pile of paper towels and toilet paper in the middle of the rest room and set fire to it. His mother tried never to let him go into a store without her, fearing he would steal something. Even when she was with him, Carl Ray usually managed to steal something, and she wouldn't know about it until later.

Fairly early in his first year in school arrangements were made for him and his mother to see the child psychiatrist recently retained by the district. The mother was to go alone the first time, then with Carl Ray. When she started talking, the long-pent-up story of a youthful affair with a young man who was later in and out of prison poured out. Once she started, she seemed unable to stop. The load had been heavy. She told how her husband, whom she married two years after the birth of Carl Ray, had promised to take the boy as his own and treat him kindly. And how that promise was broken almost immediately after the marriage. The step-father was brutal to the boy, even breaking one of the child's fingers during a beating.

She admitted that Carl Ray lied and cheated and stole things— and that she was unable to control the boy, especially since she worked full time as a waitress. After her confessional, which she considered as sacred as that in a Catholic church, there was a moment of silence. Then she heard noises beyond the glass partition—evidently shuffing of feet, a stifled cough. The sounds could be heard easily, since the glass did not extend to the ceiling.

"There are people out there!" she said in alarm. "They've been listening to me!"

They were doing more than listening—they were watching. She knew nothing about what are generally called one-way mirrors, or sometimes two-way screens. Of course the ordinary mirror is one way—you look at it and see yourself looking back. But there is a special kind of glass, or screen, that permits those on the outside to look in while those on the inside can not look out.

The young woman flung open the office door and looked out. There sat a group of people—the school principal, a student nurse, several medical students—assembled as an audience at her confessional. The young woman glanced back inside and could see the psychiatrist, who had got up from his desk and was walking toward the door.

With a piercing scream she rushed out of the office and vanished. This was too much. This was inhuman, monstrous, incomprehensible. She took her son out of school and refused to send him back until she was promised that there would be no more visits to the psychiatrist. Then she was induced to put Carl Ray in a play therapy class. Something *had* to be done with the boy if he was to stay in school.

And so it came to pass that the Carl Ray problem was unloaded on me a few days after he entered my school. All I was supposed to do was rebuild a structure that had been shattered. Still worse, I tackled the job without even knowing about the one-way mirror episode. Actually it is not unusual in psychiatry, particularly as a means of helping students. But the psychiatrist *must* inform the person he is to interview and *must* get that person's permission, not always an easy task. That school psychiatrist took the easy way.

Mrs. Barber, the mother, was so suspicious of me when I first called at her home that I got practically no information. I talked to Carl Ray but made just about as little progress. He seemed restless, uneasy, furtive, and he carefully avoided giving me direct answers. A real problem child who *had* to have help—if only to keep him from burning the school building down. On my second visit the mother told me a bit more, but her bitterness about the incident she related was strong, blocking much hope of that approach—psychiatric therapy—in dealing with Carl Ray.

The school people, after promising to keep the psychiatrist away from her and Carl Ray, persuaded her to enter the boy in a play therapy class. The little children worked with colored clay and paints. True they did smear clay and paint around a lot, even on themselves. But the theory was that it gave them a feeling of release and maybe achievement. Finger painting it's called. Another perfectly acceptable technique if practiced by trained or closely supervised persons, and fully understood by the parents but . . . In the mind of Mrs. Barber, finger painting was an insane idea. She was a waitress, always dressed neatly, and she always brought Carl Ray to school in neat, clean clothes. She accepted Middle-America values even though she could not live up to them. But the customers she served were Middle-America.

"They turned those little children loose with some big papers on the floor and pans of different colored paint of some kind," Mrs. Barber said. "The kids tried to see which one could spread the most mud . . . on everything, on all their clothes. I had to bring Carl Ray home and change his clothes and wash them while he washed off. I didn't understand. I still don't know why they wanted the children to do that."

"It seems to help many children," I said. "Ordinarily play therapy is either done by, or recommended by, a psychiatrist."

When I mentioned psychiatrist she flinched.

"Is something wrong?" I asked.

"Don't you know?"

"Know what? I don't know what you're talking about."

"You go ask that school nurse at the other school, where Carl Ray was last year. Or some other people there. I don't want to cause trouble, but you go ask them."

I did. And learned the truth. I was shocked and bitter. But you gain nothing by fighting battles of the past. My job was to help this boy. How could I do it when the mother flatly refused to let anybody in psychiatry even talk to her boy? And if there was ever a problem child, Carl Ray was one.

So I went back to the home, and when I walked in I pulled back the drapes, raised the shades, and opened the windows. Mrs. Barber was puzzled.

"I found out what happened," I told her. "I want you to know that I am not a psychiatrist and I am not a psychologist and because of that I may not be able to help you much. But I don't work tricks on people with one-way mirrors. What you tell me will be used for your benefit and with your knowledge. I hope you can feel free to talk to me, even though I might not be able to help you as much as I would like to."

The frightened young woman managed a smile. "Yes, I think I can talk to you," she said.

"I will work with the classroom teacher and the principal and with Carl Ray," I said. "But what I can do to help the boy depends mainly on what happens right here . . . and if something isn't done . . . if he sets another fire . . ."

"No psychiatrists and no mud splashing," she cut in.

"Okay, I'll do the best I can. Maybe the best start is a talk with you and your husband together. Will you arrange it?"

She said she would.

Roger Barber was a middle-size man of about thirty-five, neatly dressed, well mannered, and, at least during the early part of our conversation, kindly. He was no outstanding intellect, but he was definitely above the median, the 100 IQ mark. He was a truck driver but did not have regular work. His wife continued working because Roger didn't make enough money to carry the load, even though they lived in a small home and had an old, small car.

I moved with great caution in the situation. I lack the psychiatric background, the training, and the experience necessary to

deal with complex family affairs where there is obvious tension
and hostility. I might even make matters worse if I said too much.

It was easy to get the overall picture. Roger, eager to marry
the pretty young woman, had gladly promised to take her illegitimate son (she told him the truth) as his own. That was *before*
the marriage. After the marriage . . . then came haunting
thoughts of the man who had been there in bed before him. And
not even married! I wasn't stupid enough to remind Roger that,
if his wife had been married, the "other man" would have been
there in bed a lot more times. By some strange quirk in the male
ego pattern, presence of a husband in bed before him is acceptable
—presence of a lover is not.

Mrs. Barber told me, before I talked to her husband, that after
she made her husband stop beating Carl Ray—following the
broken-finger incident—the boy's step-father acted as though
the boy did not exist. "You should see him play with little Nancy,
our own child," Mrs. Barber said. "And all the time little Carl
Ray is watching, feeling all alone, real sad."

So I asked the step-father, "Do you think you might learn to
like the little fellow and help him? He needs a father desperately,
and you're his only chance."

"Well . . . maybe . . ."

"He's lonely," I said. "That's why he does bad things—so
people will know he is there. Sometimes a little child has no other
way of making grown people know he is there. He needs a
father."

"I guess I might try," the man said.

"I'll do everything I can at school," I told him.

"He's a liar and a cheat and a thief," the step-father broke in,
flashing anger for the first time.

"He's that way because he has no idea of what will please you,"
I said. "He wants to please you . . . wants you to be his father.
Maybe if you give it a try . . ."

I got no promise. But I began getting results—some quite unexpected, even startling. The following Monday, Mrs. Barber phoned me. She was quite excited. "Guess what? Roger took Carl Ray on a fishing trip and they both had fun. The little fellow was glowing when he got home, and he even said Daddy . . . the first time."

Strange how two males, without tensions that can build because of the presence of females, are likely to work out a pleasant relationship. I started to caution Mrs. Barber not to expect miracles but decided not to.

And there was progress at school. "He seems to be learning the difference between cheating and not cheating," his classroom teacher told me. "He's getting a fairly good idea of what truth means . . ."

"I wish I knew what it means," I said.

She looked puzzled for a moment, then returned my smile. Like Mrs. Barber, she was too enthusiastic. I knew. You don't get the miraculous personality changes, not even in little children, in real life that you get so often on TV. It takes time and patience and struggle to "overhaul" a character, especially one way out in left field. But I didn't warn . . . I just hoped.

I knew that Carl Ray was slowly learning a little about truth and honesty, and about not setting any more fires, because I had a conference with him once a week, and we had begun to talk freely about all those things. I even explained to him that to many people stealing was considered just fine—Comanches stealing horses, for example. I also explained to him there were no Comanches or horses around the school, and that the only thing stealing would do in our school and town was cause trouble. No medals.

Then it was Christmas time—and the tree came a-tumbling down.

Mrs. McCall, Carl Ray's classroom teacher, came busting into my office to tell me the glorious news. "It's Carl Ray," she said, a bit breathless. "He has donated the Christmas tree for the class. It's lovely . . . big. Come and see it. The other children are decorating it now, and after we have our Christmas party we are going to let Carl Ray take his tree home with all the decorations on it. For his own Christmas party."

Gloom started settling over me. I got up and walked wearily to the room and watched the children working on the Christmas tree. It was big—it was huge. Maybe I was wrong. The children were decorating it, making a lot of noise, having a lot of fun. Carl Ray stood surveying the empire he had built—he was KING.

Back in my office I sat meditating for a long time. Should I or should I not? I decided that I should. I called the mother. "They're decorating the Christmas tree that Carl Ray gave the class," I said.

"Christmas tree! What Christmas tree?"

I was right. "Don't you know that Carl Ray . . ."

"Oh my God!" she broke in. "And just when everything seemed to be so much better." After a pause, during which I could hear sniffling, she said, "Don't tell his father."

"I won't, but I think you should," I said. "If you are going to build a solid family structure . . ."

"I'll tell him," she said.

The person I had to tell was the classroom teacher, and that was a task I dreaded. But I told her, and after the initial shock she understood and admitted that we still had a real problem child on our hands—one that needed psychiatric help, which he might never get. Maybe all of us—teacher, social worker, parents —could do the job. There was no guarantee.

However, I was really cheered up by the denouement of the Christmas tree episode. For Roger Barber, when he was told about the theft of the tree, sat down and had a friendly talk with the boy. Maybe the incident did more than anything else could have to bring the two together. The step-father finally realized, I think, how desperate was the boy's need to attract favorable attention—to have friends.

The step-father took the boy to the lot from which the tree had been stolen. I'll never understand how that little seven-year-old lugged that big tree off without being caught. But, as Dickens clearly explained, never underestimate the seven-year-old thief. The man who owned the lot said to forget it. He hadn't missed the tree, and if Carl Ray gave it to the class, well, that was a fine show of Christmas spirit. So Carl Ray could still have that Christmas party and be King, with his tree there? No. The mother and step-father and classroom teacher and I agreed that Carl Ray should lug the tree back to the lot, which he did. I do not advocate rewards for thievery, even if the Comanches did.

Some pleasant and unexpected changes took place during the rest of the school year. Not only did the step-father quit mistreating and ignoring the boy, but he also began taking Carl Ray on fishing trips regularly. And slowly the idea seeped through to Carl Ray that there were ways of establishing friendships other than stealing and setting fires and cheating and lying. By the end of the school year he was talking to me a lot about things that, "My Daddy and me" were doing and going to do. It wasn't just Daddy—it was *my* Daddy.

The family moved away during the summer and I wrote on Carl Ray's file: "Closed—with plenty of reason for hope."

Black Executioner

"I'm worried sick about my boy Lem," Mrs. Jackson told me.

I had gone to the Jackson home to check on the family's application for free lunches for the seven children who were in school. There were five others not in school, too young. Judging by the ages of the children, I assumed that Mrs. Jackson was about forty-five (the youngest was two). She looked much older.

"What trouble is Lem having?" I asked. "I've heard no complaints about him at school. The principal seems to like him."

The principal, who had the "good" old Anglo name John Smith, had asked me to go to the Jackson home and had said nothing about Lem. For reasons not clear to me at the time, the principal seemed eager to get the children in this family on the free lunch program. The reaction I usually had from this principal was the opposite—keep the "moochers and freeloaders" off the dole.

Mrs. Jackson explained, in a quiet voice reminiscent of Negroes of an earlier era, when "black" was an insult and no Negro dared talk of freedom and equality. "Well, ma'am, a lady came by here with her boy and said Lem beat the little fellow up. Bloodied his nose and cut his lip. He was just a little boy, a Mexican. I told them Lem was a good boy and wouldn't hurt a fly. He wouldn't do a thing like that. Of course Lem ain't as bright as some boys, and I know that. But he wouldn't hurt a little boy half his size."

"What did the little boy's mother say?" I asked.

"She said at school they put boxing gloves on Lem and that little boy and that Lem hurt the boy real bad."

Boxing gloves. This must have taken place in the gym—and with school personnel on hand. I knew the physical education instructor, Graham Steele, let the boys box at times. But Lem was sixteen and big for his age—he was practically a mature man and a tough one physically. He was two years behind in his school work and most of his classmates in junior high were boys who weighed from forty to sixty pounds less than he did. In fact, I couldn't think of one boy in the entire junior high who might possibly hold his own with Lem. This was very strange.

Lem was what we call a slow learner—an I.Q. level in the upper 70's or low 80's. School psychologists have long bemoaned children in this IQ range as being in a "never, never land," for rarely do they get the help they need to succeed in school. If the IQ score is lower, the children can qualify for state-authorized special education classes for mentally retarded; if the score is higher, they can generally adjust to the standard curriculum demands of regular courses. Little has been done for the student in between the upper and lower levels of learning ability.

Lem had been advanced to the ninth grade solely because of

his age and size, and even there he was out of place, judged by those standards.

I knew the boy. I had helped him with his school work as much as I could. Results were not very rewarding—set reasonable goals when you're dealing with slow-learning children. If he ever got into high school, which was doubtful, he might become a star on the football team. So what was he doing bloodying the nose of a little boy—and in the gym? Lem could hurt a small boy seriously. But not deliberately—he would have to be operating under instructions from someone. Who would give such instructions?

I got little more information from Mrs. Jackson. All she wanted to do was what the old-time "Darkie" (a word I've always hated) wanted to do—stay out of trouble. Her husband was a garbage collector, and he took the same attitude—stay out of trouble. No talk between them about such frightening things as equality.

One of her big regrets, she told me, was the closing of the little Negro school near their former home. Few Negroes lived in the district she mentioned, so the little school building was plenty big for all the black kids. When pressure was finally exerted, a dozen years after the 1954 Supreme Court desegregation order, the little school building was closed. And things weren't too bad. The black children, being few in number, didn't encounter too much hostility when they moved in with white and Chicano children. It's in the districts where blacks make up half or more of the total population that you can expect trouble, for numbers give the blacks a feeling of solidarity and confidence—and the whites less confidence in their "superiority."

Yet Mrs. Jackson longed for those "good old days" when her children were in a school of their own, just as many people long for the "good old days" when, they forget, there were no hospitals and you sat and watched your child die if it contracted diphtheria.

I filled out the necessary forms for the free lunch program, and the principal seemed delighted that I recommended putting the whole covey of them on free lunches. This began confirming my suspicions. Soon I learned more, much more. But I didn't barge bull-headedly forward to get the story, because at that time there was quite a bit of factionalism within the faculty in preparation for a coming school board election. I couldn't be sure which teacher or administrator would tell me the truth. So I let Rolfe, a graduate social work student I was supervising at the time, do some scouting.

Rolfe and another graduate student—Manuel, the old reliable —had already expressed astonishment at the manner in which discipline was maintained in the junior high run by John Smith and his assistant principal, Barty Bernard. It was like nothing I have ever heard of in any other public school since the birch rod went out of style, soon after the turn of the century. In all other schools, the kids break free when they emerge from one class-room and head for another, which they do six times a day at that junior high. It is a momentary relief from the silent regimen in the classroom, and the kids race around and make noise. Not in our junior high. The children walked single file, two-way traffic —and as silent as the tomb. Student monitors watched and jerked out of line any child who said a word or failed to maintain the prescribed distance—two paces—between himself and the children before and behind him.

I had checked into this earlier in the year and learned that Smith had been a drill sergeant in the army, then a football coach until ulcers *forced* him to become a principal. Actually, any successful football coach can become a principal any time he wants to, as I will explain later. I checked still more, but quietly, when reports reached me about other disciplinary procedures that seemed quite extraordinary in the latter part of the twentieth century. Barty, the assistant principal, would snatch a bus ticket or a cafeteria ticket from any child who committed even the slightest infraction of what came to be known as Smith's Law. So the child might go without lunch—and walk home.

Also there was quite a ruckus in the school when Barty and a woman teacher took a thirteen-year-old girl into Barty's office and took turns whipping her on the behind with a paddle. Her crime: she giggled in class. Violated Smith's Law. "Whip her until she breaks!" Barty was saying, as the woman teacher took her turn with the paddle. The girl didn't break. Instead she became hysterical. I learned from the nurse that the girl was menstruating at the time and was in a highly emotional state even before the beating started. The nurse, who was called in, took the girl home.

And I got, on a promise of absolute secrecy, what one man teacher considered an explanation of Smith's Law. "He's impotent," the teacher said. "Can't do any good at all with his wife. He's under a doctor's care, taking some of those 'manhood pills,' but they don't seem to be doing much. And I've heard from several people that he's got a stack of porno pictures locked in his drawer. Takes them out and drools over them . . . but even that doesn't do him any good when he gets home."

"Are you sure?"

"No. But if you're hunting for an explanation of the way he unloads frustrations in a brutal manner . . ."

"I think I understand," I said.

I finally got the Lem story from Rolfe, my assistant, and at first I refused to believe it. "I figured I'd just sort of ease into the gym and see for myself," Rolfe said. "Better than getting somebody else's version, for right now, with the election coming up, you get all kinds of versions. Lem is the executioner—the Black Executioner, they call him."

"Executioner!"

"That's the word they use—kids call him that, even the little Mexican boys who have a devil of a time saying executioner. Any time a kid gets out of line, the principal and that crummy assistant take him to the gym. I don't think Graham [the gym instructor] likes what's happening . . . but he won't go against the principal. They put the gloves on Lem and on the boy that is to get some discipline knocked into him—maybe a kid weighing fifty pounds less—and tell Lem to work the kid over. It's inhuman—monstrous. Lem didn't want to hit the little kid, and he looked pleadingly at the principal. Smith just said 'give him a lesson he'll remember.' So Lem hit the kid and knocked him sprawling. The boy got up real slowly and was standing, well, sort of sagging. Lem was looking at him, terribly sorry for what he did. 'He's standing up—hit him again!' Smith shouted. 'But Mr. Smith . . .' Lem started, in a sad, begging kind of voice. Smith cut him short. 'Hit him again or I'll put on the gloves and work you over.' Of course Lem wouldn't even try to defend himself against the principal . . ."

"I know," I said. "Lem's family are still Negroes—not blacks."

"So he hit the kid again and knocked him flat. There were two other little kids waiting their turn to be knocked sprawling, but I couldn't stand it any more. I had to get out of there to keep from puking—or knocking hell out of that principal."

We sat silent, still reluctant to believe.

Then Rolfe said, "What are you going to do?"

"You know I have no authority in matters of school discipline," I said. "And there's no use going to the superintendent. He'll back the principal—I guess it has to be that way."

"How about the school board?"

"I don't think they'd even listen to me . . . and if they did the superintendent and the principal would see to it that I'm not around come September."

"I'm not going to be here in September anyway," Rolfe said. "I think this thing ought to be busted wide open, and I mean now."

"Give me two or three days," I urged. "I'll see if I can work it out."

"Okay. But I haven't even told you the whole story. You go see what he's doing to the rest of the kids. Gets them all in a circle around the ring to watch, and when blood flows or a little boy is flattened, the kids shout with glee. He's making bloodthirsty monsters out of them. Kill! Kill!"

"Cut it to two days," I said.

"All right."

First I verified, via the grapevine, that Smith would be advanced to the senior high at the end of the school year, which wasn't far off. So Lem, if he was still in school, which I doubted, would have a different principal. He was failing dismally—no chance of being advanced to high school.

Maybe I could work out a compromise. You learn to hate the word in time, but you aren't doing the kids any good if you're not there—and if I indulged in the luxury of a direct confrontation with the principal at that moment, considering my mood, one of us would have to depart. Chances are it wouldn't be the principal.

Rolfe had somewhat different ideas—not as much patience with what I called the long view. Perhaps some change in the teaching theory in schools of social work was taking place. But what he told me was inhuman—enough to make some kind of change necessary.

I drove to the Jackson home. Both parents were there, but they said little. And Lem quietly answered questions.

"Couldn't you just pretend to hit those little boys hard?" I asked.

"I tried that, ma'am. Mr. Smith said if I didn't knock them down he'd work me over."

"Well, just try not to hurt any boy badly the next few days," I said. "I'm going to see if I can change things."

I was mulling over the situation at my office the following morning when Rolfe phoned. I told him I had learned that Smith would be at the senior high the following school year. Only two more months and Lem would be free.

"Oh yeah?" he said scornfully. "I've got some news for you. Smith is taking Lem with him to senior high ..."

"He can't. The boy is failing everything ..."

"You think the principal can't advance a boy if he wants to?"

I knew he could. "You win," I told Rolfe. "I'm going out to the home again, just to check, then I'll arrange a conference with the president of the school board."

"The parents could file charges," Rolfe suggested.

"You go try talking them into it. They might say yes, just to please you, and then they might take flight from the whole district. Those parents are scared ..."

How prophetic my comment was. For as I drove up to the Jackson family home I saw that everybody was busy, loading things into two trucks, getting ready to flee. "We just had another man come here—a white man, not a Mexican," Mrs. Jackson explained. "He said Lem had beat up his little boy and he brought the boy along. His face looked pretty bad. He told Jacob—that's my husband—that if Lem touched his little boy again he was coming here and would beat Jacob until he couldn't work for a week. He was a big man, and when Jacob tried to tell him that Lem didn't want to hurt the little boy, the man just got madder and madder. We're leaving and right now." And they did.

I drove by the home the next morning before going to school ... just wanted to be absolutely certain. No sign of life. Then I went into the principal's office. "I just came by to tell you that a family has moved out of our district, so you can mark the children off the rolls," I said.

"What family?"

"Lem Jackson's family," I said.

"Lem!!!" The principal came up out of his chair. "Why he can't... that's impossible..."

"They're gone. I just drove by the empty house."

"But why?"

"The mother told me some of the school people had put boxing gloves on Lem and made him beat up little boys—discipline. The fathers of the little boys began going to the home and threatening to beat Mr. Jackson into a pulp. One father was there yesterday —had his little boy along to show..."

Smith sat and stared at me but said nothing.

"The Jacksons are Negroes of the old school," I said. "All they want is to avoid trouble. They won't fight back. So they took flight."

"Where?"

"The mother wouldn't tell me... but they're out of our district. I know that."

The big principal sort of sagged back in his chair. He was shaken—perhaps not so much by the departure of Lem as by the knowledge that I knew what had happened, and that maybe quite a few others knew.

A bit later I called Rolfe and told him what happened. He was disgusted because I didn't take him along for a direct confrontation with the principal. "Somebody ought to tell him . . ." he started.

"Somebody did," I explained. "I did it my way, and I have an idea it will be even more effective in the long haul..."

"Maybe you're right," Rolfe agreed. "Just makes me wonder if I'll last out my first year of social work."

"I think you will," I assured him. "And I also think it's real fine that you feel the urge to protest vigorously . . . and will do it when that's the best way. This time I don't think it was."

I had one more talk with the principal after that—another checkout. He seemed older, less vigorous. Seemed to be living under a cloud of some kind.

Then there was a new principal at the junior high in September. And he came to me to see if I could help him "cure" an after-effect of Smith's Law. "I told all the kids to quit that goose-stepping business in the halls," the principal said. "But they sure had that drilled into them. The seventh-graders learned it so well last year, when they were being ordered around, that they are enforcing it on the younger children. I can't get them to stop."

I suggested that the younger children wouldn't put up with it long, since there were no orders from above—and they didn't. In a month or so the children were moving along the hallways in a free and easy manner, talking, having a breather.

Battle of the Broken Teeth

Rudy peered out at the world with what seemed to be a permanent expression of alarm, like a squirrel peering out of a knothole in a tree in times of danger. He looked that way because he always held his right hand over his mouth. The result was strange. Even his heavy black eyebrows seemed to be constantly raised, adding to the impression of alarm.

Rudy was the son of migrant Mexican-American farm workers. The family—there were eleven children—usually hit the migrant trail the first day of May and did not return until the first week of October, which meant two months' loss of school time for Rudy. Added to that handicap was the language barrier. He knew no English when he entered first grade, and progress since than had not been significant, partly because only Spanish was spoken in the family, and the family was on the migrant trail so much with other Spanish-speaking people. And now the squirrellike peering out at the world.

A favorite stopping place for the family while on the migrant trail was Florida. The lure of the orange harvest. Florida orange trees are old and tall, lovely to look at, especially when laden with golden fruit. A ladder must be used in harvesting oranges from upper branches. Rudy fell from the top of a ladder, where he had no business being, since he was only a child. When he fell, his mouth struck the bottom rung of the ladder and his two upper front teeth were snapped off midway between the bottom of the teeth and the gum.

Chances are there is a workman's compensation law in Florida that would have required Rudy's employer to have the tooth damage repaired. Such laws seldom furnish justice to Mexican-American migrant laborers, who usually don't know what their rights are. Even if they know they may be reluctant to take action. It is fate. Since the days of the Aztec rulers and on down through centuries of Spanish and then Anglo domination, the attitude of the Mexican-American laborers has been pretty much the same. Let fate take care of things. Only recently is this attitude changing.

So Rudy held his right hand over his mouth, and he did it for two reasons. The broken teeth were ugly. "Other kids make fun of them," he told me. And the teeth caused constant pain because of the exposed nerves. Sometimes Rudy pressed quite hard on his upper lip, as though deliberately lacerating it on the broken teeth. Perhaps one pain compensated for another—spread the pain and you can endure it.

The boy was two years behind in school work and doing poorly, even though tests showed that he was capable of passing. His chances of staying in school were not good—no good at all unless something was done about the broken teeth. I decided to make that Project I. I talked to Betty, the school nurse. "My own

teeth begin hurting when I watch him," I said. "Can't we do
something?" I also explained that he might make considerable
improvement in speaking English if he would take his right hand
off his mouth. "Most of the time I just get a mumble from him,"
I said. "Teachers can't understand very well even when he is
pronouncing English words correctly."

Betty tried . . . and ran smack into that dreadful jurisdictional
block. There was a dental clinic that would do restorative teeth
on children, without charge to them. But Rudy was fourteen, a
year too old.

"He doesn't look more than ten," I said.

At the adult clinic Rudy could get his teeth pulled . . . that's
all. So Rudy could, if he chose, exchange his broken teeth for
empty gaps where teeth ought to be.

"The teeth hurt him constantly," I told Betty again.

"I know," she said. "He comes to the clinic asking me to help.
I can't even give him an aspirin . . . I would be charged with
practicing medicine."

The only reason Rudy was still in school was because Manuel
Campos, the graduate student I was supervising, tracked the boy
down and brought him. But Manuel was not hopeful about keeping Rudy in school. "The broken teeth, the language barrier,
time lost on the migrant trail . . ."

"I thought they provided schooling for migrant children," I
said.

"Are you kidding? Sure, they try, and they have two or three
so-called model layouts that they put on display. But they don't
try to force a thirteen- or fourteen-year-old boy to spend time in
school when the family needs the money he can make. I even
had trouble locating Rudy," Manuel continued. "The parents
live in the Wayland district, not ours . . ."

"Shhh . . . not so loud," I cautioned. Children whose parents lived in another school district were not supposed to attend school in our district. But among the migrants, with their big families, shuffling children around among relatives was so common that school people generally ignored it. Trying to "unshuffle" them for school purposes would lead to chaos—and things balanced off, anyway.

Rudy lived with an aunt who did live in our district. She had quite a family of her own, yet she took the boy in. "I feed him and give him a place to sleep and keep his clothes clean," she told me. "What else? He's my nephew." The clan structure is far stronger among poorer Mexican-Americans than it is in Anglo Middle America—because of the combination of large families and poverty.

Rudy took full advantage of his dual residence. He would tell his mother he was going to school in our district and tell his aunt that he was going to school in Wayland. Quite often he didn't go to either. He roamed the streets, first giant step toward delinquency.

It is easy to name the areas in which the public schools do not measure up to perfection in educating children and helping to develop character. But a check of the early dropouts, or kickouts, reveals a solid case for keeping the child in school, a part of the generally approved way of life.

What baffled Manual, who had attended schools in Mexico until he reached the college level, was the apparent indifference of children in this country. "There must be something wrong," he said. "You go into a classroom in Mexico and you find the children eager, responsive, almost radiant. Here they act like the whole thing is just a bore. And the Mexican-American kids especially. They just sit there, glum, feeling neglected, maybe resenting it."

I don't know anything about schools in Mexico, so I didn't argue. The best I could do was concentrate on individual cases—

trying to keep children in school and trying to help them adjust
and develop a desire to learn. I did caution Manuel about one
thing, and I felt an obligation to do so, since I was supervising
him. "Remember you're dealing with plenty of Anglo kids . . .
don't use Rudy as a means of satisfying resentment you might
have against Anglos. You won't even help him if you do that.
Sure, it would be better if we had more Spanish-speaking teachers and social workers and so on in this part of Texas. But where
are you going to get them?"

Manuel meditated.

"You get them by helping these Mexican-American kids stay
in school and go on to college," I said.

"I see what you mean," he said. "I guess I was getting a little
too emotional about things . . . after all, you work for the Chicanos
just as hard as I do."

"And also for the Anglo kids who need help . . . and you do
that too," I reminded him.

First thing we did was arrange for Manuel to spend a half
hour a week with Rudy trying to improve the boy's English . . .
and helping him in math, which he couldn't seem to handle. But
we continued to work on Project I, getting those teeth repaired.
I decided that if I arranged to have the mother enrolled in a man-
power training course for migrants, the pay for this training
might be enough to finance the tooth restoration job. What happens? The mother breaks her arm the first day at the school.

But Manuel was reporting some progress. "Since he can't think
in the abstract in English—has to think in Spanish and translate
—I've started teaching him math in Spanish," Manuel said.
"He's catching on. Then when he learns English better he can
make the transition."

Finally we hit pay dirt in what Manuel and I had started calling the Battle of the Broken Teeth. The principal, a Catholic,
and I were able to persuade a Catholic clinic to have its volunteer
dentist do the work without charge. And the tooth job was started.

Rudy passed my office every day when he changed classrooms, and on the final day of his visits to the dentist I was waiting for him, expecting a radiant boy flashing a smile so I could see his fine new teeth—and no hand over them. But he was holding his hand over his mouth tighter than ever when he approached me. And he was trying to hold back tears that wouldn't be held back.

"Rudy, come here," I called, when I noticed that he was going to walk past me.

He came near.

"What's wrong? Didn't you get your teeth fixed?"

He didn't say anything because he couldn't. He held out a tear-stained slip of pink paper. "I have to leave," he muttered, moving his hand a bit—enough so that I caught a glimpse of the fine restored teeth.

"What do you mean you have to leave . . ." I started. Then I glanced at the slip of paper. I had seen such slips before, many of them. This was a checkout slip. Rudy had to leave the school system.

"I have to go to all my teachers and get them to sign the paper," Rudy said, and again he moved his hand enough to expose the new teeth. They were fine. But were they to be a sign of victory or of defeat?

"How many teachers have you checked out?" I asked.

"All but one. And I wanted to stay. Since Mr. Manuel has been helping me I am learning. My friends are here."

"Don't check out with that last teacher," I told him, taking the pink slip to be sure he couldn't. "You are still in this school as long as you haven't checked out with all your teachers. And you're going to *stay* in this school. Come with me."

I took him into my office and got the whole story, verifying it by telephone to be absolutely certain about procedure. A classroom teacher, an Anglo who didn't know one word of Spanish and who had, inadvertently, revealed to me her dislike for Mexican-Americans, had, for reasons that I still do not understand, been placed in charge of the school's migrant labor program— all Mexican-Americans. Betty, the school nurse, had gone to this woman, a Mrs. Sanders, during the campaign to get Rudy's teeth repaired.

Mrs. Sanders had checked with people at the migrant labor office and learned that Rudy's parents did not live in our district. He lived with an aunt in our district, but she was not his legal guardian. As I have said, shuttling these Mexican-American migrant children about with relatives is routine. So bingo! Mrs. Sanders went to the assistant principal, not the principal, and he agreed with her that Rudy should be dropped from the rolls of our district. Let him go to school in the district where his parents lived.

I was positive that the principal would go along with me and have the drop order revoked immediately. But he was out of town, attending a convention. So I went to the assistant principal. I confronted him with the tear-stained pink slip—the facts. "When did Mrs. Sanders get the authority to decide who goes to school in our district and who does not?" I asked.

"She doesn't . . . but . . . but . . ."

"But you let her drop this boy without saying a word to me, when you know how hard I have been working to help him— and just when we finally managed to get his teeth repaired so that he might have a chance, especially with Mr. Campos tutoring him."

"But the rules . . ."

"You kick the boy out and that's the end of him," I cut in. "He won't show at that other school. He's had too many defeats— he will abandon hope . . ."

"But the rules . . ."

"Do you know that Mr. Gray [the principal] has known for two years that this boy has been living with an aunt?"

"No, I didn't know anything about it until Mrs. Sanders showed me the report. Legally he . . ."

"Do you know that there are more than a hundred children, mostly migrants, in the Wayland district that legally belong in our district?"

"Why no . . . I had no idea . . ."

"And do you know the kind of wild confusion we would have here if somebody presented Wayland school officials with a certified list, from the migrant worker office, of all those children of ours that they are teaching?"

"Why who in the world would ever do a thing like that?"

I looked at him and smiled. It wasn't a kindly smile—he got the message.

I didn't have to go to the principal. After he returned from the convention, he got the "message," as I knew he would, and called me in. He knew the story of Rudy.

"I think his best chance, maybe his only chance, is to stay with us as long as we can keep him," I said. "I don't think he would bother to show up at Wayland."

"We've had him two years, I see no reason why we can't have him a few more," the principal said. Then he added, "Just for the record, so nobody can cause trouble in the future, will you get the family to sign a statement that the aunt is presently the child's guardian?"

"Sure," I said. I knew that Manuel could get the family to sign anything he wanted them to. Well, let's say he could get the mother to make her "X" mark—she couldn't write.

Manuel set off with a fancy-looking document, the kind you see in the world of officialdom in Mexico, and returned with the "X" marked in the proper place—plus the stamp of a notary public.

Rudy was getting along fine during my last year with the

school. Only on rare occasions, when he was suddenly embarrassed, did he forget and put his hand over his mouth, covering
those fine new teeth. Manuel had left, his MSW clutched tightly
in his hands, and Rudy was being helped by another graduate
student I was supervising, a big, fair-haired Anglo named
Whitlock.

That's the way Rudy wanted it. When Manuel left, I offered
to arrange for special tutoring, without cost, by a woman who
spoke English and Spanish with equal fluency. Rudy said no.
"This is my country and I am an American," the thin little end
product of the migrant trail said. "I've got to learn English real
good and write it and talk it the way other people do." Then he
added, to my surprise, "Anyway, Mr. Manuel used a lot of big
words in Spanish that I don't know. He doesn't speak Spanish
the way we do."

I saw Manuel a year or so later and told him. He was delighted and a bit flattered. Manuel speaks the kind of Spanish you
might hear on the campus of the University of Mexico. But the
Spanish of the Texas-Mexico border country, sometimes referred to as *pocho*, is quite different. Many English words have
been absorbed and changed in ways that puzzle Mexicans south
of the border country. Rudy spoke *pocho*. But I'm sure that by
now he speaks pretty good English.

Damon and Pythias, 1

After a clash with the teacher—and clashes were becoming routine—Damon, age eleven, left school early, saying he was going home.

"Go home and don't come back!" the exasperated teacher told him.

He didn't go home. Instead he managed to steal from a grocery store a large bag of candy and proceeded to eat all of it. Damon was an accomplished thief. He was also a diabetic. After gorging on forbidden sweets, as he did frequently in spite of heroic efforts to guard him, he was likely to go into a coma unless he had a shot of insulin. When he went into such a coma and did not have his insulin, there was a chance that he would never come out of it alive unless medical aid was received in a matter of hours.

When he failed to return home from school that day, his parents, who said they were missionaries, called police, firemen, radio and TV stations, newspapers, and friends. Soon the great child hunt was in full swing. The entire city set out to save Damon.

Some service men from a nearby military base noticed the boy lying in a ditch. It was then 4 A.M., and Damon, after complaining to the teacher that he felt sick, had left school at 3 P.M. the previous day. The service men carried the boy to the military hospital, and doctors there were able to bring him out of the coma. But they said that another hour's delay might have been fatal. As soon as Damon was able to sit up in bed and notice things, he asked if he could see the newspaper. Ah, there it was—his picture on the front page and a big story about the massive child hunt. He smiled weakly but happily. The objective was achieved—the world knew about him.

Damon was a character disorder, a term psychiatrists and psychologists use, not always accurately, to classify people who simply do not fit and for no reason that seems to make sense. So-called compulsive liars are usually lumped into this category. Add diabetes to character disorder, then add a companion character disorder, Pythias, and you have a situation without parallel. That was the problem unloaded on me, but in this situation I politely but firmly refused to assume all responsibility. Others had to help me.

Of course the names of the boys were not Damon and Pythias. I made the connection because they were almost inseparable. They roamed the streets together, indulging in offenses against the generally accepted pattern of life. Damon was delighted at the opportunity to train his new-found friend in the finer points of juvenile delinquency. Particularly stealing.

Dealing with character disorders is a rugged undertaking, because even they do not always know where truth leaves off and fiction begins. If a complete fabrication brings a favorable reaction, the character disorder continues telling the story—and finally thinks that it is true. And many people in this classification are charmers. At least on the short haul. A distinguishing characteristic is that they begin to fret under an enduring bind —except with another character disorder or a quietly dominating wife or husband. But quite often they are able to make professionals who are trying to help them—in this case probation officers, social workers, teachers, even psychiatrists—look like monsters.

Damon completely charmed the juvenile probation judge. Furthermore, the missionary parents had influence with the judge. So that worthy jurist, looking at the sweet, innocent little boy, ignored the advice of professionals again and again and sent the boy back to the foster parents.

Far more than half the cases referred to me concerned children neglected or abused by parents or foster parents. Overaffection can be even worse. I ran smack into it in trying to deal with Damon. This boy might die unless some drastic change was made. And by drastic I mean taking him away from the missionary foster parents and putting him in a controlled environment. Actually, they had managed, because of friendship with the juvenile judge, to get him out of just such a controlled environment—an orphans' home. But even it wasn't controlled enough. When Damon sneaked down into the kitchen at night and was found stuffing jellies and jams into his mouth with his hands, the psychiatrist recommended a far more rigidly controlled environment. But the juvenile judge, with those radiant missionaries offering "a home of his own with love and affection," turned the boy over to them.

The routine continued. "That's a fine boy," the judge would say, fingering his key ring. It was a lovely key ring—Damon had made it especially for the judge. The charmer. "He's got what he needs," the judge would say, "love and affection and a home he can call his own." Back to the missionary trap. The father held a good-paying job, and the mother's missionary work was confined almost entirely to overmothering Damon—or hunting for him.

Even principals and teachers were slow in facing reality in Damon's case. He was always neatly dressed. He was a good-looking boy. Even the little gap between his two upper front teeth set off his charm, like a mole, real or artificial, on a woman's face. The boy had straight shoulders—just a clean-cut, all-American boy.

When his foster mother, a champion talker, began telling me the story, Damon wandered out of the office. The character disorder frets under restraint of any kind. Mrs. Davis said that she and her husband were missionaries of some small religious sect that I don't recall now. Evidently their missionary work was confined to Project Damon. "We enrolled Damon under our own name because he needs to feel that he belongs, that he has a home of his own and is loved," Mrs. Davis said.

"He isn't your real son?" I asked, surprised. No one had told me the boy was adopted—well, he actually had not been adopted. Thank heavens, juvenile court still retained custody.

"His family name was McKnight," Mrs. Davis said. "His father abandoned him when he was a baby, and his mother began running around with other men and neglected him. They put him in an orphans' home—and we managed to rescue him and give him a home he can call his own."

"If he lives that long," I was thinking. "What about the little one?" I asked, pointing to the squirming baby in her lap.

"He's ours. But we thought we should do more. Remember, we are missionaries."

The thoughts that came to my mind then turned out to be correct. The foster parents, determined to sacrifice to the bitter end for Damon, turned out to be the toughest roadblock in the campaign to save the boy. And I mean just to save his life. The missionaries didn't mind *any* sacrifice for Damon. Normal human beings *do* resent demands for unusual sacrifice, and on that point they are right. Sacrifice beyond the point of reason results in mutual hatred. And so Bettelheim was right—love is not enough.

I explained to Mrs. Davis that I refused to assume responsibility for what Damon ate, which she asked me to do. "I have many other children to consider," I said.

"It's that classroom teacher," she started . . . I quit listening.

A simple test that I use with children who appear to be emotionally confused told me a little about Damon:
   If he were a bird, what kind of bird?
   A blackbird—few children would pick such a bird.
   What kind of animal?
   A deer—flight?
   What kind of insect?
   A scorpion—the sting of death, probably self-inflicted.
I sensed in the little fellow a wish to gorge to the limit and get the show over.

Damon asked to be transferred. I explained that a transfer would make no difference—the only problem was avoiding sweets.

If this boy was to make any kind of adjustment, he *must* have help in the nature of a rigidly confined environment, insofar as eating sweets was concerned. It was clearly obvious, to everybody except his foster mother and the juvenile court judge, that Damon could not make it on his own. With such control, there was a good chance he might adjust and eventually lead a useful life. Character disorders are quite competent in those areas of human activity in which no contact is maintained for long—in selling used cars, cemetery lots, and such. And many make good spouses, in a situation where the mate exercises almost complete control, but in such a way as to leave the opposite impression—part of the make-believe world the character disorder creates for himself.

So I refused to transfer Damon. Then came the massive child hunt. And after that the shattered plate-glass window. And, at last, action.

Damon and his disciple, Pythias, were roaming the streets as usual. Mrs. Davis wasn't worried this time because Damon had taken his insulin and needle along—sneaked them out, she said. Just when the boy learned to give himself insulin shots I never learned. Evidently when he was quite young—when his real mother began neglecting him. And it is possible that gorging on the forbidden sweets was, in a way, compensation for that neglect. So when he had his insulin and needle along, Mrs. Davis did not worry. And on such forays, which might last three or four days, he did some rather amazing things.

He convinced one couple that his mother had deliberately run him away from home and told him never to come back. They took him in. He ate all the sweets in the refrigerator that night, took an insulin shot, and departed. But throwing the brick through the plate-glass window of the bakery—that was too much. The police were on his trail this time, following him and Pythias. They saw Damon throw the brick through the window. By the time they reached him he was already stuffing pie into his mouth with both hands.

"My father ran off when I was a baby . . . my mother left me for other men . . ."

Back to juvenile court. At the insistence of Glenn, the probation officer on the case, the judge reluctantly agreed to have the boy temporarily confined in a hospital while psychiatric tests were being made. The diagnosis was what any intelligent person familiar with the facts expected: Damon should be placed in a controlled, structured environment and kept there for observation and psychotherapy until a decision could be reached about future procedure. The state hospital for the mentally ill was willing to take the boy for a period of observation and therapy. I had a good idea what that meant—the period of observation and therapy might be long.

I started to close my file. But I was forgetting something—the sacrificial foster mother. She came to my office, pleading this time instead of complaining and denouncing, as she usually did. She begged me to send a report on Damon to the state hospital. "He is in the hospital under our name," she said. "We're using our hospital insurance to cover the cost of the examination. If you will make a report, I think we can get him out of the hospital and back home where he belongs—where he has love and affection . . ."

I sat staring at her in disbelief. She still wanted to sacrifice to the bitter end, even if meant death for Damon. It was incredible. For a moment I was tempted to unload on her—to blast her out of her smug feeling of infinite virtue. But I've come in contact with the closed mind many, many times, and I know that reason and logic have no place in the picture. I told her I would write the state hospital. I did *not* tell her what I would write.

I told the hospital director that I was writing solely because the foster mother had begged me to. I told him that, on the basis of the psychiatrist's report and my own experience with the boy and the foster parents, I felt absolutely certain that Damon would not be alive in a year if he were returned to the foster parents. I agreed strongly with the psychiatrist—controlled environment.

Then I marked Damon's file closed and turned much of my attention to his little pal, Pythias.

Two years later I saw Damon, quite by accident. He said he was in a school for boys and was doing fine. "There are fifteen other boys, and a preacher runs the school . . . but he's not a missionary," he said. "He's just an ordinary preacher."

"How about sweets?" I asked. "And your insulin?"

"The people at the hospital gave me a lot of stuff that tasted sweet but didn't hurt me," he said. "And I got to liking people and did better."

"You still take insulin shots?"

"Yes. I take one every day," he said.

"You like the new home? The boys in it?"

"It's all right," he said. "I don't have any trouble."

No pressure—no leaning—no claims on him. The character disorder can seldom stand up under the strain of continuing demands of a close personal relationship, but quite often he makes a fine adjustment to the more casual relationships that exist in a structured environment—the military, for example.

"Do you ever see Mrs. Davis?" I asked.

He hesitated, then said, "No, ma'am. The people at the hospital told me not to."

So Bettelheim, you win. It was impossible for Damon, who never understood the meaning of love when he was a child, to survive when it was suddenly showered on him—by strangers. He escaped by taking flights. Now nobody demanded love from him. Limited goals can, at times, bring nice rewards.

Damon and Pythias, 2

The Pythias family had been evicted from their home—father, mother, and seven children out in the yard looking at the piled-up, junky furniture and other belongings. The Christmas tree brought to the home by an older daughter who was an exotic dancer lay on its side. No lights blinked. It was Silent Night—without the uplifting effects of music.

But for Col. Anthony B. Green, retired, it was a night of glory. For five long years he had battled to get the Decker family, alias Pythias, out of the home he had mistakenly rented to them. Victory at last! Colonel Green had little time in which to revel over his triumph. On New Year's Eve he died of a heart attack. Perhaps the five-year ordeal with the Decker family had been too much for one man to bear.

The Deckers emerged smiling. The father, who usually acted slowly, if at all, moved in a hurry when he saw the family belongings being piled in front of the house. And before Christmas Eve was over, the family had settled in a nicer home. They bought it—paid two hundred dollars down.

In moving they crossed the line between the two elementary schools on my list; so when the holidays were over, I faced the task of trying to fit Pythias into a new setting—different principal, different teachers, different children. I dreaded it, for Pythias was, as I have said, a character disorder. Even though he was only ten, the trouble he could and did cause was remarkable. My primary objective was to get him to school and keep him there, for all kinds of other problems—stealing, malicious mischief, breaking and entering—developed from his activities when he was not in school, and that was quite a bit of the time.

There was, however, one consoling factor. By that time, Damon, pal and leader of Pythias, was no longer with us. Pythias had deliberately hunted up Damon and established the relationship. Now and then when Mrs. Davis, foster mother of Damon, toured that part of the city while hunting for the boy, she would stop at the Decker home and ask if they had seen Damon. Pythias became interested. This must be an exciting boy. So he sought out Damon and became his follower.

Psychiatrists would probably have classified almost all members of the Decker family as character disorders, from the alcoholic father on down the line. And they were what I call happenees, a breed of people I have mentioned before. The father would stumble from small-pay job to small-pay job, and in the process of stumbling he might wind up with a metal plate in his head. Or a broken leg.

"I had a good job driving a truck," he told me, "until I had that accident. They put this silver plate in my head. Feel it." I felt it. Happenee. "After that I couldn't get my license back, so I been working in that feed store. Them sacks is heavy and the pay sure ain't much. And now I'm laid off. But there's a job at a feed store across town . . ."

While driving the ancient family car, the mother ran over their baby. It fell out and a wheel passed over its head. "I think maybe I hurt his brain," she said, as she held the squirming, crying year-old child in her lap during my first visit to the home.

The oldest son, now married with three children of his own, ran over a boy on a bicycle and killed him. Decker junior had no driver's license at the time, so he had to switch jobs. Now he seemed to be doing all right, the mother said, as a roofer on houses. Give him time . . . he'd fall off.

The father did—and broke a leg.

The oldest girl, the exotic dancer, was in trouble with the law now and then over custody of her children.

Pythias fell and broke an arm. Breaking bones seemed to be a speciality of the Decker family. The little boy cried for two days and nights, complaining that his arm hurt. The father, drunk at the time, finally sobered up enough to take the boy to a doctor. The arm was broken. Because of the delay, it didn't heal neatly. "Feel them bones," the mother told me. I felt the bones.

Pythias stayed away from home often, sometimes for two or three days. He stole things, slept in abandoned houses, and at times broke things for the sheer joy of breaking them. Even the six-year-old girl, Jean, in school for the first time, would stop at the dime store on her way home and do a little shoplifting. She was learning the technique from Pythias.

The younger children were bed wetters. They didn't restrict their wetting to beds but would foul up the furniture or the floor. I noticed dampness on the sofa where I was sitting and moved. I couldn't escape the odor of urine.

There seemed to be no pattern in such procedures as eating

and sleeping. A hungry child would open a can or a jar and start digging out the food. His dinner. This disorder could probably be attributed in part to the threat of eviction that hung over the family for five years. And the mother was not physically able to handle the household properly because she was pregnant most of the time. Colonel Green swore she got pregnant just to avoid being evicted. Under Texas law, a pregnant woman can not be evicted.

The telephone company cut off service in the middle of a conversation I was having with Mrs. Decker. Before that I asked her to call me if anything needed my attention, and she usually said, "I will if the phone ain't cut off." It was. There were threats of cutting off the water, but the health department saved that day.

The father evidently drank large quantities of beer. He usually ignored Pythias at such times, the mother said. But when there was no money for beer and the long-drawn-out hangover got a grip on Decker, he would become irritable and beat the boy.

The mother was defeated—no other word describes her attitude. A product of the Piney Woods of East Texas, she had known nothing but hardship. She tried to escape by marrying when she was only fifteen. Then came the succession of babies, two of them stillborn, two that died in infancy. The word *faded* described her and the dress she wore, and if she had another dress I never saw it. The one she wore was shapeless. It would yield to pressure as she grew big with child, then sag back after she delivered.

"I don't know what to do," was her usual response when I presented any aspect of the Pythias case. And since the boy's name was not Pythias, I'll switch to what his mother called him, Johnny, to avoid confusion. "I don't know where Johnny goes and what he does," she said. "His Daddy sorts out the lunch money for the three of them every morning, but Johnny doesn't go to school and he stays out until late at night sometimes."

"Why not let the girls carry the lunch money and give Johnny his share at the cafeteria?" I asked.

"Oh, his Daddy wouldn't want that," she said.

"Couldn't you do it?"

"I don't ever get my hands on no money," she said. "Andrew never tells me what he makes or what he does with the money . . . he never gives me any . . ." The character disorder demonstrating his manhood—his *machismo*. And in this case the wife lacked the strength to be dominant, even by indirection—a situation that isn't so good when the husband is a character disorder.

"Well, you tell your husband that we will have to file charges against him if Johnny doesn't come to school," I told her.

"He won't pay no attention to anything I say . . . acts like he don't hear me."

"Maybe he will pay some attention to this," I said, handing her an official warning. "You give him that and see what happens."

The first thing I had noticed about Johnny, alias Pythias, was that he moved faster than anybody I ever knew who had no place to go. He was a young man in a hurry. He was small for his ten years, chubby but not fat, and his ears and cheeks shone red, as though freshly scrubbed with a rough cloth. His eyes were fringed by heavy black lashes, adding interest to his appearance. And he was a charmer, even when he was blandly telling me an outrageous lie and I knew and he knew that I knew. I think Johnny would have felt that he was slipping if I ever "caught" him telling the truth. I didn't very often.

He was so young that it seemed possible to change his goals, his set of values, his techniques of making life serve him. You can't always be sure. Some children, waifs on the streets of Rome not long after World War II, became fixed in their values and ways when they were only seven or eight. Yet some as old as thirteen or fourteen can be changed, but not often.

I had conference after conference with Johnny—and still wasn't sure whether I was getting through. But on one point I was sure. I was being pressured by the principal (worried about his precious ADA) to keep the boy in school. Or file charges against the father.

"Let me make one more visit to the home," I said. "If I can't do any good this time, I'll file."

At the home I found that things had changed—for the worse. Decker had been fired from his job at the feed store across town because Colonel Green kept dragging him away from work and into court on the eviction proceedings. When Decker was out of work, he was out of beer. He got mean then, and suddenly he loosed one of his outbursts on the school. He stormed into the principal's office saying that Johnny had been locked in the school building overnight.

How can school officials prove that a boy wasn't locked in a school building overnight? It's like asking a man to prove that he has led a virtuous life. The principal was shaken—all thought of filing charges against Decker were delayed until the "atmosphere" was better. No principal wants to get up in the morning and read a headline, "Child Locked Overnight in School."

By the time we had decided to proceed with charges against Decker, the family moved again—bought another house. As I expected, Johnny never bothered to go to the Garden Elementary School, the one he was supposed to attend. After five days I filed a charge against the father of violating the compulsory school attendance law, even though I have always been reluctant to file such charges if the parents are poor. What can you gain by fining a father who can't pay? What do you gain by putting him in jail so that he can't work?

Well . . . what you gain is his attention. And in a hurry. The majesty of the law deeply impresses parents in such situations. There is an old saying that motivation is often inspired by the pull of hope or the push of discomfort. The push of discomfort caused the father to get Johnny back in school in a hurry, and promise to keep him there.

But what about the pull of hope? In one way or another, it

was up to the new principal and new classroom teacher and me and a few others to see if we could furnish that pull of hope. Otherwise I knew Johnny's stay in Garden Elementary would be fleeting. So we set out on a Pull Plan—something that might possibly give the little boy an objective, a limited one, at the school.

We were going to give Johnny some special-assignment work —something he would consider a job. Such special-assignment work can be a blessing or can turn into a curse, depending almost entirely on the principal. It often works wonders if the child is *permitted* to work as a favor—an "assistant" in my office or in the library, for example. This works with bright children. Results can be extremely unfortunate if children not so bright are, at least in their minds, *forced* to do such special-assignment work as cleaning up the playground. I've seen this done by many principals as a form of punishment—and sometimes the boys are called "Dummies" by other children. Where there are different ethnic groups, the attitudes of these groups must be considered. A Mexican-American boy is likely to flatly refuse to work in the lunchroom, considering it woman's work. He will go without lunch rather than do such work. Yet a boy such as Johnny . . .

"Johnny, how would you like to have a job here at school?" I asked him at our first conference after he showed up at Garden Elementary.

"But they wouldn't want me," he said.

"They might. You just get all slicked up in the morning, ready to put in your job application."

He was polished, shining. I took him to the principal. "We've come to see if you might need some help in the lunchroom," I said. Of course the principal and I had rigged everything in advance, but I didn't want Johnny to know that. I wanted *him* to take the initiative. "This is Johnny Decker," I continued. "He would like to apply for work in the lunchroom."

Johnny just sat, looking surprised.

"Go ahead, Johnny," I urged.

"Could I get a job in the lunchroom?" the boy finally said. "I work real fast." If he worked the way he moved when he had no place to go and nothing to do, the lunchroom manager would be able to dispense with other helpers.

The principal was deliberately businesslike. "Well, I'll need a boy who is strong because there are heavy things to lift in that lunchroom," he said. "And we need somebody who is dependable —who will be there every day without missing once. If a boy misses once without a good excuse, he can't work there any more."

"I'm strong," Johnny said. "And I won't miss a day."

"Let me feel your muscle," the principal said, leaning forward and feeling the little arm as Johnny flexed his muscle. "Hmmm . . . pretty good muscle," the principal said.

"And I'll be there every day," Johnny said, beginning to show enthusiasm. Motivation can be inspired by the pull of hope . . .

"Of course you'll get paid in a way," the principal said. "Your lunch will be free . . . and you can pick what you want . . ." The pull of hope . . .

"I'll be there every day," Johnny said.

"We'll give you a week's trial," the principal said. "If you do all right, you can have the job."

Johnny was there every day, moving trays around at what I considered an alarming pace, although he seemed never to drop anything. And he was, at last, beginning to use some of his potential in the classroom. He was making good grades and causing no trouble. Things *had* to work this time. As they say in the space program, this was the "window" necessary for blastoff. Scrub the mission and there might be a long, and possibly unhappy, delay before another window opened.

Johnny really blasted off in that lunchroom. In a short time he was throwing his weight around among the other children who helped. They worked only one day a week—he worked every day. The principal and the cafeteria manager had agreed on that plan when I explained the importance of this first move to pull Johnny into the general pattern of school life.

Then Johnny got enough confidence to go out for the school baseball team. In the past he had watched occasionally but that was all. He made it—became the team's pitcher. One day I stopped and watched when he was pitching. And I thought, "That pitching arm . . . that's the one that was broken . . . I felt the rough place where the bones had knit . . . there are other scars you can't feel or see . . . maybe, just maybe, they will heal . . . I'll take the mended arm as a symbol . . . maybe next the mended life . . ."

The last day of school Johnny came into my office and told me he wouldn't be back in September. There were tears in his eyes. "I like it a lot here," he said. "Only school I ever liked."

"What happened?" I asked.

"We're moving away," he said. "And just when I passed with good grades and was having fun working in the lunchroom . . . Mrs. Haines said I could work there again in September . . ." Mrs. Haines was the cafeteria manager.

"Johnny, they'll have a cafeteria in the school where you go," I consoled. "And they'll have a baseball team and you can pitch."

"How did you know I pitched?"

"I watched you."

He was delighted.

"People will do nice things for you if you'll let them," I continued. "I'll bet some day you are manager of your own cafeteria."

"You think I could be!"

"I'm sure of it." The pull of hope. But what else? The push of discomfort is often necessary in dealing with adults. It seldom produces gratifying results in dealing with children.

I drove him out to the family home to tell them goodbye. It was another "Silent Night"—the Deckers had been evicted—again. "We couldn't make them payments," Mrs. Decker explained. The old, faded dress sagged. No longer could she develop a bulging midsection to evade eviction.

The old, faded furniture and other belongings were being loaded on Decker's ancient pickup truck and a much bigger truck owned by a cousin who lived in the Piney Woods of East Texas. The cousin had come to rescue them—to take them back home.

Santiago on the Rooftop

Negotiating with Santiago, age six, wasn't easy, because he was on top of the chicken house and I was on the ground. And he wouldn't come to the negotiating table unless the enemy, which I symbolized at the moment, capitulated completely. That is, agreed that he did not have to go to school. And if you are wondering how there happened to be a chicken house in a thickly populated residential area of San Antonio, bear in mind that the barnyard chicken still figures in the lives of many poorer Mexican-American people in the Southwest.

Fortunately, I had reinforcements, even though Santiago's mother was of little help. As the Mexican-American male begins building a feeling of equality among men, one of his first acts is likely to be a declaration of independence from the centuries-old matriarchal system. Among most deprived, repressed peoples—

blacks in this country, for example—the mother represents what stability there is. Along with stability goes authority, even though it may be exerted indirectly.

So the mother was losing her matriarchal bind on her children, and she had to call in the two older girls. They were willing and eager to help. They climbed onto the roof and captured Santiago, dragging him to the negotiating table. There he stated his case. I saw that there was a measure of logic in it. Why should he, age six, be forced to go to school when his nine-year-old brother, Juan, did not go?

I had never heard of "Juanito," as the family called him. He was a wheelchair case, a victim of polio. His legs were withered. Three years earlier his father had taken the boy to school to enroll him. Although the father could get along moderately well in English, he became confused when Miss Stevens, the principal, started telling him about another wheelchair case.

The cases were not parallel. But Juanito's father was not able to understand the difference. The earlier wheelchair case, an Anglo boy, required considerable special care. The boy's back had been broken in a traffic accident, and he was paralyzed from the waist down. He had no bladder or bowel control. He couldn't move onto his chair or off it. His family had the means to furnish the needed help, however. So he went to school.

Juan's father was a day laborer. There was no money to pay someone to help Juanito. Santiago was only three and the older children, the girls, worked. And so Juanito's father took the boy home. There he spent most of his time wheeling around the house and listening to the radio. Or he looked at the few old magazines and occasional newspapers that were brought into the home.

The mother was illiterate and could not help him learn to read. But he did get some help from his older sisters and his father, both in learning English and in learning to read that language. His mother, an immigrant, spoke no English.

When the time came to enroll Santiago in school, his father

took him, even though it meant time off from work. The mother was reluctant to go because she could not speak English. Santiago asked the principal why he should go to school when his older brother didn't. The principal said that Santiago had to go to school because he had to go to school and that was that. Early indoctrination into the democratic processes.

Santiago decided that the reason was not sufficient. He took flight. Once he reached home, he climbed onto the roof of the chicken house. When the girls got home from work they hauled him down, and the following morning his mother took him to school. Santiago had to translate for her, and there is no way of knowing how literal or accurate his translating was. At any rate, as soon as his mother left, he set sail again. That time he headed for the Rio Grande. The rooftop didn't seem to be an enduring sanctuary.

The six-year-old boy had no idea that the Rio Grande was 150 miles away. All he knew was that many Mexican-American people, including immigrants like his mother, talked a lot about "going back home." And to them home meant Mexico. With the rise of the Chicano, many Anglos began urging all Mexican-Americans to do that—love it or leave it. But the Chicano has decided that this country, not Mexico, is home.

Santiago had underestimated the iron will of Miss Stevens. She got in her car and set sail after him. Out on the highway to the Rio Grande she stopped him and drove in front of him. She got out of the car and tried to grab him. Miss Stevens could outrun Santiago, but catching him was something else. A greyhound can easily outrun a rabbit, but operating alone the hound seldom is able to catch the rabbit, which darts sideways and backtracks too quickly. So greyhounds hunt in pairs. Miss Stevens was operating alone. Santiago would elude her and start backtracking. She would get in her car, when she was almost exhausted, drive in front of him, then get out and start the chase again.

The strange spectacle attracted the attention of two Mexican-

American women in a passing car. They sized up the situation quickly, whereupon the driver pulled up beside Santiago and the other woman opened a door of the car. There is no need to speculate about what happened next. The little Chicano leaped into the car and the women drove away, leaving the blonde "enemy" standing and shouting. The women drove Santiago to his home and instantly he climbed on the chicken house roof—barely in time, for Miss Stevens was really aroused by then. She finally abandoned hope of coaxing him down—and I was called in to tackle the job.

"I don't know how you are going to talk to him," Miss Stevens told me.

"He speaks English, doesn't he?"

"Quite well, all things considered. But when I followed him home—when those two women took him home—he climbed on the chicken house roof and wouldn't come down."

"I'll see what I can do," I said.

Miss Stevens made no mention of the crippled older brother, which seemed strange—and still does—since she was principal at the time Juanito was brought to school.

So we had a family powwow at the home. The older sisters not only translated for their mother, but they also stood guard over Santiago to keep him from heading for the rooftop again. Juanito wheeled his chair up close to us. Listening from the other room he realized that he was the central subject of conversation, so he decided to take part.

Could he feed himself?

He could.

Did he have bladder and bowel control?

He did.

Could he move from his chair to the commode and back without help?

He could.

"Would you like to go to school?" I asked Juanito.

"I would like it very much," the boy said.

"Will you go to school if Juanito goes?" I asked Santiago.

"Yes ma'am."

I make no attempt in this writing to capture in letters the sound given some English words by Spanish-speaking people who do not have perfect command of English. But teachers comment occasionally that almost all children brought up in Spanish-speaking homes say "jez ma'am," instead of "yes ma'am." The teachers also note that a young Spanish-speaking child is also likely to say "jez ma'am" to a man, and this is considered hilarious. I find no humor in it.

The father came home from work then, and I thought of something he might do to help Juanito at school. Could he make a thin board that would fit across the arms of Juanito's chair. This makeshift desk would help the boy in writing and in other ways. The father said sure. He had a friend at the army base where he worked, a carpenter's helper, who would make the board. There are thousands and thousands of Mexican-American and Negro carpenter's helpers in South Texas, very few carpenters.

We still faced the problem of transportation. The father could take Juanito to school but did not get off early enough in the afternoon to pick him up. A possible solution came to me. Now and then this family hit the migrant trail to build a little stake for lean times in winter. They seldom went far, working mainly at stoop labor in the farm area surrounding San Antonio. But they had been on the trail the previous summer—they *were* migrants. Our schools were supposed to inform adult migrants who had children in school that they were eligible for training—mainly English, reading and writing—and would receive thirty dollars a week during the training period.

Not all adult migrants, however, were informed of this. I made a point of telling the mother, the girls translating for me. "If she goes to the migrant training school, she will have enough money to pay someone to take Juanito to and from school," I told them.

The mother said that she would go—and that they had a neighbor with a car who would transport Juanito to and from school.

I said nothing to Miss Stevens at the moment, preferring to give her vague answers when she asked about Santiago. A parent or guardian must accompany a child to school to enroll him— or to get him back in school after he has been out for several days. If I showed up with two warm little bodies—Juanito and Santiago —plus a parent, it would be difficult for the school people to reject either of them. So I herded the little group—father, Juanito, and Santiago—into Miss Stevens's office.

She was quite reasonable, especially when I explained in detail how the crippled boy would be able to care for himself. "You're both in school," she told them, smiling. Then she looked at Santiago, pretending to act mean, and said, "And I don't want to be chasing you out that Laredo highway anymore. You understand?"

"Jez ma'am," Santiago said.

In a surprisingly short time Juanito became something of a pet in the school. The other boys would grip his wheelchair and go storming down the hall, shouting "Gangway."

Juanito was riding Cloud Nine—with neither foot touching the ground. He rewarded the other boys by letting them take rides in his chair. They got a big kick out of it, but they couldn't maneuver the way Juanito did. And the other boys would assemble on the sidewalk when it was time for Juanito to be delivered, then push his chair at a rapid clip to the building, work it up the steps, and sail on down to his room. Even the man who brought Juanito to school and took him home seemed to derive pleasure from his job over and above his pay—which came from the thirty dollars a week that the mother was being paid at the migrant school.

On one memorable occassion when Santiago showed at school early and spread the word that the man couldn't bring Juanito that day, the other boys took over. Santiago was too little to push that heavy chair all that distance. But he had a small army of helpers, and soon here they came, a few minutes late but victory achieved!

All very rewarding to me. And my joy was even greater when Juanito was advanced to the second grade at mid-term. He was a bright boy and had learned to read fairly well before he came to school. And the little crippled boy warmed my heart many times. If I was in the hall when the other boys were pushing him rapidly along, he would always point to me and say, "That lady did this for me."

One day Juanito told me that his mother wanted to know if I would come to the family home some afternoon.

"Is there any trouble?" I asked. "Santiago is doing all right, isn't he?"

"No trouble," he said. "She would like for you to visit."

And so I visited. The mother asked me to sit in a little chair beside a table on which there was some paper. Juanito was near-by and Santiago soon came into the room, demanding his share of the limelight. I knew that all the attention being lavished on Juanito caused Santiago to feel a bit jealous at times. It's that way with adults as well as children—even if the attention goes to a cripple. But Santiago had his satisfactions, including pushing the chair now and then without any helpers. Shared responsibilities—a feeling of being needed; and he could feel that way because he was never ordered or forced to push the chair.

"I make mark for name," the mother said, speaking English slowly and carefully. She made her mark—X—the way she had always signed her name in the past. "Now I make my name," she said. She wrote her name. Actually, she drew, or printed, it, the way little children do in learning to write. "See!" she exclaimed. "My name. I no make mark now."

I told her it was all quite wonderful. The joy of learning. And, tragically, all too many of us deliberately quit learning at a certain "stage up the ladder," assuming, incorrectly, that there is no need to learn more.

I glanced at Santiago and thought he felt more left out than ever, now that his mother was replacing his brother as the center of attention. "Do you ever climb on top of the chicken house any more?" I asked.

"No ma'am," he said. "I like school. I am learning fine. You are a fine gringa lady."

The word *gringo* is usually flung with scorn. But it can have connotations of affection, just as can *bastard* and *son-of-a-bitch*. There was no mistaking the affection in the "gringa" that Santiago bestowed on me.

I closed the file and marked on it, "Another reason for never giving up the battle."

The Chocolate Kid

Jeannie's mother was Mexican-American. And even though Texas law classifies both Mexican and American Indians as Caucasians (white), Mongoloid features (hair, skin color, facial bone structure) were quite obvious in the mother. Jeannie's step-father was a blond Nordic. Swedish ancestry. And Jeannie?

"I'm chocolate," she told me. "I'm the only chocolate one in my family."

She would not use the word *Negro*. And *black* had not replaced *Negro* at that time. It still hasn't among many of the older Negroes of the South. But it was impossible for the child not to know, since her black hair was kinky. The head hair of most Negroid people curls tightly on the scalp because each hair is flat on one side. The hair of most Mongoloid people is usually round—straight hair. The often-curly hair of Caucasoids is likely to be oval.

"Pressing" is the term used to describe the process of straightening the kinky hair of Negroid people. But the term and the practice are fading out, now that "I am black and beautiful" has become current as part of the liberation of black Americans. And the so-called Afro hairdo or haircut is put on display with pride, even arrogance in some cases. Pressing had not faded out when I was called to the rescue of the teacher who seemed unable to meet the challenge of Jeannie, age nine. Even though there were some blacks on the faculty, there were no Afro hairdos or haircuts.

Worst of all, in Jeannie's case, she was left to guess at the cause of her "tangly" hair. She was not told that she was half, or maybe a quarter, Negroid. The other genes came from her Mexican-American mother. Nor had the girl been told that she was illegitimate, although she undoubtedly wondered, since she was five years old when her mother married the blond Swede and there was never a word about any previous husband.

When I come face to face with tragedy inflicted upon a child because of the stigma of illegitimacy, as I have many times, I wonder if it would not be wise to adopt the policy of those nations which permit an unwedded mother to name a "husband," even though she picks a name at random.

So in the mind of Jeannie came the same disturbing question again and again: Who am I? She could establish no satisfactory identity. And although I moved slowly and said little when I began talking with her, I was convinced that the child's problems were not likely to be solved until she had some satisfactory answer to that question: Who am I? True, the revelation might shock her. But one recovers from a shock, whereas uncertainty may haunt for years.

I set forth on the difficult task of helping Jeannie establish identity. And the situation was complicated even more because Jeannie had genes from all three major root stocks—Mongoloid, Caucasoid, Negroid. The chances are a thousand to one that her father was not a "full-blooded" Negro, as people used to say. The males who owned ancestors of today's black Americans spread Caucasoid seed generously—often forcefully. Then there also is evidence, in the opinion of most competent anthropologists, that the Mexican Indian has some Caucasoid genes.

Now and then I read some comment by an anthropologist that the most beautiful people on earth are those in whom the three major root stocks are blended—in some Pacific islands. Very nice. But try to sell Jeannie a bill of goods along that line and see how far you get. Especially when you add the fact that she was illegitimate. You can understand the nature of the problem I faced.

Jeannie's answer was hostility, often expressed violently. To herself she might ask "Who am I?" but to others—principals, teachers, children—she established her identity quite clearly. She was the one who shouted and fought and intimidated. She was the one they would notice.

Jeannie's classroom teacher was an Anglo male, and he was ready to give up the battle. There are more men teachers in elementary schools now than in the past. The ancient saying that "a teacher is a man who can't get a job or a woman who can't get a husband" no longer holds true. In fact, school administrators often seek out men teachers on the theory that they can deal better with boys. Perhaps they can, but quite often they are frustrated in dealing with a little girl who is a firebrand.

Jeannie was so aggressively hostile that Clark, the teacher, was beginning to talk to himself. He was a pretty nice guy, reasonably competent—and held no race prejudice. But Jeannie was something out of a different world, in his opinion. So I was called in.

I could get little information from the child in our first interview . . . except what I hear so often, "Everybody hates me . . ." and so on. I decided to face that attitude head on. "Are you sure everybody hates you? Have they told you? Have you ever told another girl that you like her? Maybe they like you but don't like some of the things you do."

She didn't seem to be listening, a defense mechanism a child develops early in life if it seems necessary. But she was doing more than listening, for at our next conference she proudly presented me a sheet of paper that she said was her survey—her Gallup Poll.

Jeannie had taken the direct approach. At the top of the page she had written, "Do you like me or hate me?" To a child there is no middle ground—no gray areas. You like me or you hate me. Under that heading she had written the names of the thirty-one other children in her classroom, leaving a blank for the answers. In each blank was an answer, in typical fourth-grade handwriting. Twenty-eight wrote that they liked her. Two girls even wrote, "I love you." Three, all boys, wrote that they hated [did not like] her. Actually, they didn't write the word hate. I had an idea those three were small boys who had been roughed up by Jeannie at one time or another.

This seemed to be the first significant triumph in Jeannie's life. And in achieving the triumph, she had demonstrated not only enterprise and ingenuity but also a willingness to face reality. Jeannie was charmed.

But there were repercussions that were not so delightful. Since she had approached all the children in making her survey, there was much more talk about her. Now and then a child would say that Jeannie was a Negro. She challenged them, something I didn't know about until later. "All right, you come to my home and see my mother and my little sister and I'll show you I'm not a Negro," she said.

They went—eight of them. They were emerging from the family home when I arrived there for a talk with the mother. And Jeannie was saying, "See? I told you my family is white."

Jeannie's mother definitely was not white, no matter what Texas law says. For that matter, I am not white—I actually have more skin color than black Americans, which shows the absurdity of that vanishing euphemism "Colored people," even though the NAACP does stubbornly cling to it. But that little three-year-old half-sister of Jeannie's was loaded with Nordic genes, for she was a blue-eyed blonde, which contrasted dramatically with Jeannie's "chocolate" color.

Jeannie had told me, before I went to the family home that day, that she thought her real name was Sanchez. Common-law marriages between Mexican-Americans and blacks in Texas have occurred occasionally—of course legal intermarriage was banned until recently.

"Why do you think your name is Sanchez?" I asked.

"I saw a paper at home one time. But don't tell Mama. She gets sick if I talk about it."

"Many children are adopted," I told her. "And a lot of them have nice homes. People adopt children because they want them."

"But I am the only chocolate one in the family," she repeated. "And a man named Sanchez wouldn't be chocolate, would he?"

"He could be," I said.

"And why does my little sister have soft blonde curly hair when my hair is black and tangly?"

"Do you remember when your mother and father got married?" I asked.

"No. I was in my mother's stomach when she got married the first time."

Obviously she had been told that there had been a previous marriage. Maybe there was one. If so, why wouldn't the mother talk about it?

"How old were you when your mother married Mr. Swenson?"

"I was five. Mama says he is my real father. I don't know. And she won't let me ask her."

Confusion. But if I barged in and tried to "clarify" the situation . . . there was no way of knowing what turmoil I might cause. I moved cautiously.

Mrs. Swenson was a small, attractive woman in her middle twenties. Her features were a little like those of the Mayas. There was little visible evidence of the Spanish genes that were undoubtedly there. The conquistadors, bringing no women with them, were extremely competent at spreading genes. One thing about Mrs. Swenson was quite obvious—she was pregnant and well along. She talked freely to me. "I am a Mexican," she said, with no show of either pride or shame.

"Is Jeannie Mexican?"

"Not all."

"She says she can't talk to you about her father—you won't let her."

"I could never talk to my mother," she said. "Maybe that's the reason I got into trouble when I was only fifteen. And my mother was so hateful all the time I was carrying Jeannie. She even made me hate the child I was carrying, and I guess I marked the poor little thing. But Harry has been such a wonderful father to her. He's overseas now, in the army, and I don't know what I'll do about Jeannie when the baby comes. My mother and sisters will be glad to care for that one . . ." She indicated the blonde child playing on the floor. "But they won't take Jeannie and she knows it."

"Have you ever thought of telling Jeannie about her real father?" I asked.

"I don't know how, especially since all my family consider it a terrible shame. Her real father was named Sanchez. He was dark, but many Mexicans are dark. I didn't know at the time. Now I know I ought to do something, but I'm afraid. I don't want Jeannie to hate me." She paused, then went on. "One time I made up my mind to tell her. But her father came back then. He scared me—he's real mean. I didn't say anything."

"She knows she's part Negro," I said.

"She pretends not to know—like bringing those children here today. I wanted to cry. But I don't want her to hate me. She thinks I neglect her because I don't help with her home work. I went to school six years, but I can't do those things . . ."

"There are college graduates who can't help fourth-graders with the new math," I cut in. "Don't let that worry you. But some day Jeannie will have to know . . ."

"I can't tell her!" the mother said.

"I know . . . not now . . . just think about it."

At my suggestion the principal transferred Jeannie to the classroom of a black woman teacher. Almost immediately the new teacher took some positive steps to build the girl's confidence in herself—to help her establish identity. Jeannie was appointed a runner, carrying messages from the principal's office to various persons in the building. Then she became the "secretary" to the principal's secretary. She was permitted to answer the telephone during part of the lunch hour. The child was responding nicely. We were making progress. But shortly before the end of the school year developments at home created genuine turmoil.

The mother became seriously ill shortly before her baby was due and had to be rushed to the hospital. The father, the blond Swede, was flown back home on emergency leave. The fair-haired child was placed with relatives of the mother. But nobody wanted the "Chocolate Kid." The step-father was willing to care for Jeannie but he couldn't. He spent practically all his time at the hospital while his wife's life was in the balance.

I talked to him. He knew all about Jeannie and had enough character and compassion and courage to accept the situation and legally adopt the little girl. Not once, as far as I could learn, did he ever unload hostility on either the mother or the illegitimate child. Such men are rare—fantastically rare if the child is both illegitimate and "chocolate," and the man a blond Nordic. Still he could not handle the situation.

By coincidence, an executive of a girls' ranch near the city visited our school to talk with the principal, whom she had known earlier in her professional work. I was in the principal's office at the time, talking about the problem of doing something for Jeannie.

"Why we have a group of girls just graduated from our school," the woman said, "and there will be room for Jeannie if she wants to join us. We can keep her part or all of the summer."

The ranch was integrated. I knew about it. Whether Jeannie was chocolate or plaid, legitimate or illegitimate, the ranch could be a temporary home for her.

The principal and I called Jeannie in and told her. The woman executive explained about the camp. The little chocolate girl was delighted, the principal and I greatly relieved. Jeannie's classroom teacher agreed to take the girl into her home, where there were three other children, during the few remaining days of school. Then came the "War of the Press"—and I'm not talking about newspapers.

The principal was so overjoyed that he made an appointment to have Jeannie's hair pressed at his expense. "I want her to look nice when she gets there," he said.

Jeannie's black teacher wasn't enthused at all. "If he sends her to a beauty shop and gets her hair pressed, then she can't fix it herself and it will look dreadful until it's pressed again in a week," the black teacher said. "All she needs is to have her hair rolled," she added. "And she has to use oil on it, not the hot irons they use in a press. She can roll it herself—I'll give her the oil."

I knew little about the obviously intricate processes of dealing with Negroid hair. The black members of our faculty had been there only a short time, and I hadn't talked to them about pressing hair. Before that I had had practically no contact with black teachers and little with black children, because of segregation.

I was a bit puzzled by the complexity and vigor of the debate about Jeannie's hair. The principal wisely cancelled the appointment for the press, choosing to let the blacks settle the issue. Jeannie had "good" hair, one teacher said. I didn't know what "good" hair was. All Jeannie needed to do was use warm combs, another teacher said. And so on and on and on. They were still debating the "Battle of the Press" when Jeannie left for camp. And I had grown weary of it and was inclined to consider it silly.

How wrong I was!! However, I thought the battle might still be raging when school reopened in September, so I decided it would be a good idea to visit Mrs. Swenson the day before the opening and check on the situation.

"My husband's leave ran out and he went to that camp and brought Jeannie back to help me," she said. "I still wasn't strong enough to take care of the new baby and the house and little Hilda [the three-year-old]. Jeannie has been a jewel," the mother went on. "I don't know how I could have made it without her. She thinks the new baby [this one had the mother's Mexican Indian coloring and features] is her toy. Plays with it and takes care of it. And is real nice to Hilda. And you know what? Jeannie is getting to be a good cook. It's all been wonderful."

"Did you ever tell her?" I asked.

"I couldn't."

"Where is she?"

"In the kitchen. She loves to work there. I'll call her."

Some day, perhaps two thousand years from now, we will relearn what our ancestors knew two thousand years ago—that a child develops into a healthy adult only if it is given a chance to participate all along in life.

Jeannie came in then—and I just sat there like a dope, my jaw sagging, my eyes bugging. She had the most glorious Afro hairdo I had ever seen.

"How do you like it?" she said, grinning at me.

"Wonderful!" I said. "Just wonderful."

Now I had to protect this child against possible traumatic experiences when she showed up at school the next day. So I told her to come to my office before she went any place else in school. I took her to the principal, and I had all my ammunition ready— I was prepared to wage war for Jeannie's hairdo if I had to.

As we walked in, the principal greeted us cordially but seemed not to notice the hairdo. I think he was sort of smiling inwardly— maybe he knew something that I didn't. "Let's take Jeannie to her new classroom teacher," he said, and away we went.

The teacher was black—but a man, not the black woman teacher who had waged the war against the press. And this black teacher had a fine Afro haircut—not wild and exaggerated, but, as Mercutio said of his wound, it served. It identified him as a black proud of his ancestry.

Child and teacher looked at each other for a moment, and I could feel the bond of human communication being established. Soon the two were chatting away, oblivious of the principal and me. We exchanged glances and left.

It was no longer necessary to answer Jeannie's question: "Who am I?" She knew—and was proud.

The Dog Trainer Moves In

"I can't stand it another day," said Mrs. Roland, the classroom teacher. "There's that big, fat forty-five–year–old woman sitting in one of those tiny seats made for seven-year-olds. And she keeps reaching out, touching the hand of her little darling." Mrs. Roland really unwound. "She distracts the attention of the other children. Some are even insisting that they bring their mamas to school to sit by them—and maybe hold hands. She's driving me out of my mind. I can't stand it any longer."

Mrs. Roland was talking to the principal and me. "It won't last much longer," the principal said. "And if you stick it out, we'll give you a medal for heroism above and beyond the call of duty."

I guess he used the expression because Mrs. Andrews, mother of the boy, was the widow of a colonel. Mrs. Roland was not impressed. "I've got her stuck in a seat where the blazing sun shines right on her," the classroom teacher continued. "She just wipes the sweat off her face and smiles and then reaches out and touches little Billy's hand. There they are, a forty-five–year–old woman and her seven-year-old boy acting like lovers."

"Hold on for a week or two," the principal urged. "We'll find a solution."

"I'll try," Mrs. Roland said.

Little Billy had school phobia, as it is generally called. People usually think that school phobia develops almost exclusively in first graders, making the big break from home into a new, and to them, alien world. It doesn't work that way except in rare cases. For one thing, the first grader isn't making as drastic a break as people might think. Even though the big-family era, during which the child had siblings near his own age, has passed, today attending kindergarten or a Head Start program—or even watching Sesame Street—helps in the transition. Within a short time first graders are having fun at school. But a child who develops school phobia later does so, usually, because of some traumatic experience—possibly a change in life pattern. Then the problem may be difficult.

That's what happened to Billy. There was no hint of school phobia during his first year at school, when his parents lived in California. His father, a retired army colonel, was proud of his boy, the last of the line, and probably indulged him a bit too much—making a sort of pet of him, since the older children had married and moved away. And Billy's attachment to his mother in those earlier years may have been quite emotional, since she was sick fairly often and had to be taken to the hospital, leaving him at home to wonder about the possibility of her dying. Many small children closely associate going to the hospital with death.

Soon after the end of the school year, Billy's first, his father died of a heart attack. The mother moved to San Antonio, into a nice apartment near the home of a daughter who was married to a sergeant. "His father made quite a pet of Billy," she told me during one of our conferences. "When his father died, Billy began clinging to me. Finally he wouldn't budge a foot from me."

I make no attempt to analyze this complex situation. I suspected immediately that the mother was "clinging" more than the boy. But it was sufficient for me to know that there was mutual dependence of a kind that was harming both—let some psychiatrist determine the nature of the dependence and suggest a remedy. My job was to keep Billy in school. And I wasn't making any headway, especially since the mother followed the pattern I have observed for lo these many years—she blamed the principal and the teacher and eventually me. We just didn't know how to handle a sensitive child. The assumption on her part was, of course, that her Billy was the only second grader in school who was sensitive. How do you deal with a sensitive child who isn't in school?

When school had opened, Mrs. Andrews brought her boy to one of the elementary schools where I worked. Billy wouldn't let his mother leave him. He clung to her skirt and began screaming when she tried to pull free. "Don't leave me, Mama," he wailed. "Don't leave me." Mama didn't leave him. She took him back home. But the story repeated itself the second and third days, and that's when I was called in. I called Mrs. Andrews and she agreed to bring Billy to my office.

The emotional disturbance was worse than I had expected. When mother and son came into my office they left the door open. "Billy, will you please close the door," I said.

He wouldn't budge an inch from his mother . . . wouldn't run the risk of being eight or nine feet from her. His mother told him to close the door. His grip on her skirt tightened. This child was in bad shape. He needed a kind of help I couldn't give him. I could visualize the situation—little Billy in bed cuddling close to his mother, the sickly mother who had been in the hospital many times. Little Billy a symbol of the man who was no longer there. Little Billy afraid that his mother would suddenly die as his father had. Mutual sickly dependence, something usually out of my field of professional work.

Mrs. Andrews launched a tirade against the classroom teacher and the principal. I listened for a time, then said, "How can you know anything about the teacher since Billy has never been in her classroom?"

She didn't have any very good answer.

"I suggest that we confer with a psychiatrist," I said.

"Psychiatrist! There's nothing wrong with Billy."

"Do other second-grade children hold onto their mother's skirts and scream when the mother leaves them?"

"But he's a sensitive child . . ."

"You think we don't have other sensitive children?"

She finally yielded, and I arranged with Captain Goodrich, the young psychiatrist at the military base, to see the mother and boy. This action gave me a feeling of relief—but oh how fleeting the moment was. Captain Goodrich called and suggested that, at least for a short time, the school permit the mother to stay with her boy.

"You mean in the classroom?" I asked, incredulous.

"Just for a short time," he said. "I think with some play therapy for the boy and conferences with the mother I can reach a solution in maybe a couple of weeks. It's a pretty bad situation . . ."

"I'll see what I can do," I said. "But that mother in the classroom . . ."

"Just give it a try," he urged.

And so I did. But it was two months before that classroom teacher forgave me. Day after day the mother was there, sitting in that tiny seat, beaming at her boy. And the teacher was going wild. And both teacher and principal were demanding that I give a firm definition of "temporary." To them it was beginning to seem permanent, although I got assurances now and then from the psychiatrist that he was making headway. Billy was responding nicely, the mother was a bit more reasonable.

I doubt if things would have worked out without unexpected help of a nature that seemed completely incongruous with reality. I had a call from the sergeant son-in-law, whom I had not met. "You want to get that boy in school and keep him there?" he asked.

"Tell me how," I said. "Tell me in a hurry, because the lid is going to blow here in a day or two."

"I can get Billy in school if you and Captain Goodrich will help me," he said.

"Keep talking, please."

"You just arrange for a powwow in the principal's office with Billy and Mama and the psychiatrist and the teacher and you and me there. You leave the rest to me."

"But how could we get Captain Goodrich here at the principal's office?" I asked.

"You ever hear of something in the military known as rank?"

"I see," I said. The Colonel's Lady.

"I can handle that boy. I'm a dog trainer."

"A dog trainer?" I was baffled.

"Sure. I train those war dogs, the ones they send out to set off booby traps so soldiers won't have to do it. The mean dogs—at least they're mean when I get through with them. You train dogs . . . well, you learn about people."

This was the most fantastic procedure ever suggested to me, but I was willing to try it. I arranged the powwow, as the dog trainer called it.

The fireworks started about the time all of us were seated

around the principal's desk, and, until she finally became exhausted, Mrs. Andrews carried on the major part of the battle, lashing out indiscriminately. I admired the way Captain Goodrich eased tension again and again by subtly diverting hostility to himself. He was an artist at it. All that time the sergeant said nothing.

When the various parties had talked themselves out, he said, in a quiet, calm voice, "You let me handle him and I guarantee he'll be at school in the morning." There was a moment of silence, and the sergeant added, "And I guarantee he'll stay there."

"And just how?" the mother asked with scorn.

"I'm a dog trainer," the sergeant said. "If I have to, I'll hogtie him and deliver him like a sack of potatoes. And if I have to, I'll stay there with my knee on his chest until he stops this foolishness."

He shook all of us, including me. It took me a moment to realize that he was being deliberately brutal in order to force the mother to face reality. Her own son-in-law hogtying her son . . . and because . . . actually she *knew* . . . the son-in-law was forcing her to admit it. "How horrible!" she said.

"Is it any worse than what's happening to him now?" the sergeant said. "Do you want him sitting on your lap and you cooing at him until he's a grown man, or do you want him to break free and start growing the way a man child should?"

"You dreadful . . . you horrible . . ." She broke down and sobbed. Nobody said anything. After a long pause, after the mother had finished her crying, she nodded approval. The dog trainer had won. Now let's see if he could deliver.

He was as good as his word. The following morning he delivered Billy at the school, pointed him in the right direction, and commanded "Go!" as a hunter might command a retriever, the only difference being that the hunter would probably say "fetch."

Billy went. I watched in disbelief as he began mingling with the other children. He looked back at us twice. Then he started playing with the children. He forgot us.

"How in the world did you do it?" I asked the sergeant.

"It wasn't easy," he said. "First I thought I was going to have to hogtie Mama. Then that Billy was screaming and trying to kick until I got him in the car and set sail. But halfway here he sort of settled down, and I think he was breathing free air by the time we got here."

I was baffled. Evidently it took a *physical* break in this situation as a base on which an emotional break—or easing off—might develop. The dog trainer was smart enough to know that. "Now you promise to keep him here," the sergeant said to me. "Or I'll stay . . ."

"We'll keep him," I said. "I will make him Project I. I've had enough of that mother pouring it on us."

For a month the sergeant delivered Billy every morning. He wouldn't trust the mother, although he was willing to let Billy ride home on the school bus, which the boy enjoyed. At the end of the month Billy came on the bus. The sergeant dropped by my office one day and asked how Billy was doing.

"Real fine," I said. "Other children like him and he's doing all right in the classroom. How about the mother?"

"Say, you'd be surprised. She's taking off some of that lard and doesn't look bad at all. She's in some kind of activities with other women—colonel's wives or widows, I guess. And my wife said she was out on a date the other night—retired colonel. That's what will cure that nonsense for good—a first-rate stud." The sergeant blushed, then said, "Excuse me, we talk that way in our dog work."

"I understand," I said.

The case of Billy-and-Mama was closed a couple of weeks later when Mama called to tell me that Billy had been picked by his classmates as best citizen in the class. "Isn't it wonderful?" she said.

"It's wonderful," I agreed, even though I wonder just what constitutes a "good citizen" in the minds of second graders.

If the "miracle" of Billy's sudden healthy adjustment seems to contradict observations I have made about the difficulty in changing attitudes and life patterns, perhaps the explanation is to be found in the fact that the boy's period of emotional confusion was of short duration. Not long enough to "mark" him.

The Prostitute Chain

As the Chicano, Mexican-American equivalent of "Black" as used by American Negroes in their own liberation movement, makes his bid for equality in the Southwest, many individuals will suffer. Even bystanders. This tragedy is inevitable in any large-scale socioeconomic revolution, and such a revolution is under way now. Occasionally the victim is a Mexican-American caught in the trap of race prejudice in reverse—he is denied relief that Anglos are trying to give solely because they are Anglos. Gloria, age fourteen, was such a victim.

Gloria's grandmother had been a prostitute in her younger days, when she could attract almost any man. As her allure faded, soon after she was thirty, she survived by living with a succession of older men in common-law marriage. She was now living with her fifth common-law husband, an elderly man who seemed senile. But he drew a monthly pension. Security. Gloria lived with her grandmother—or was supposed to.

Gloria's mother, almost a stranger to the girl, was a prostitute. She seemed to have no permanent or semipermanent home. Finding her usually involved visits to a number of bars.

I was called in on the case when the principal found a switch-blade knife in Gloria's locker. The principal told the bus driver about the knife and suggested that he keep Gloria seated across from him in the front of the bus, so he could watch her. Then the principal and I visited the grandmother. She appeared to be about seventy but was probably in her early fifties. And she spoke no English. The old man living with her seemed unaware of what was going on. Gloria did the translating and quoted her grand-mother as saying that she would see to it that Gloria was at school every day from that time on. But Gloria wasn't at school every day from that time on.

This was a case for Manuel Campos, my graduate student in social work, and he was pleased to tackle Project Save Gloria— that is, save her from a life of prostitution. Manuel was a bit more realistic in this area, since prostitution is legal, although restricted to certain areas, in Mexico—and he knew that the number of productive years of a prostitute were about the same as those of a professional athlete in this country. About ten. But the prostitutes in Mexico start their careers younger, at thirteen to sixteen, and are usually washed up in their middle or late twenties. Gloria was fourteen, which would be considered the ideal age in Mexico.

Manuel began losing some of his enthusiasm in dealing with the case after two fruitless days of hunting Gloria's mother. The best he could do was leave word at various bars. And, surpris-ingly, she showed up at his office in response to one of the messages. I saw the woman—thin, frightened, and shopworn even at twenty-nine. And I heard some of the conversation. The partition between my office and Manuel's was thin. But I heard only the mother, who spoke in English. Manuel's voice is so soft and low it does not penetrate walls.

"I'm so ashamed and so scared," the mother said. "My mother has always had her way, and I'm afraid of her. She is stronger. I guess that's why I . . . I started living the way I do. It was the way she lived . . . and I never could talk to her. But please, Mr. Campos, try to save my little girl. I know I've never done anything for her. My mother wouldn't let me . . ."

Manuel spoke softly. I didn't hear what he said.

When the mother left he came into my office and told me the story. "Gloria stays out all night with boys, sometimes gangs of them," he said, "and sometimes with grown men—for money. She's getting a good start on the prostitution trail."

"The prostitute chain," I suggested. "Do you think you can break it?"

"What do you think?" he countered.

"The only hope is to get her into some school for girls for two or three years. Maybe she could learn some other trade or profession."

"You're not hopeful?"

"Should I be? You've been through some of these court battles with me."

"Well, I'm going to try," Manuel said.

His picture of prostitution did not exactly fit the situation in this country, where the ancient profession is illegal. He visualized the situation in Mexico—if prostitution is legal, the demand for youth is so great that older "athletes" are sad, abandoned figures even before thirty, whereas a woman in her forties who has a moderately good figure and is clever might get along fine in this country. Still . . . both of us took a gloomy view of prostitution as a path to the better life, whatever that might be. And we carried on the Save Gloria project.

"I don't think we'll win," I told him. "The chain is too strong —the old grandmother too tough. But I agree that we should try." Of course my job was to keep Gloria in school—or try.

First it was the switchblade knife. Then it was a raid by the narcs on an abandoned home where a gang of youngsters, including Gloria, were suspected of blowing pot. No pot was found, but we at school were duly notified. Then it was absenteeism with no excuse. Then came the carbuncle on the butt. The case was becoming a burden on me because I had to go with Manuel every time he went to the grandmother's home to bring Gloria back to school. "I don't want to be with her alone," Manuel said. He was right. Careers of some school men have been ruined by gossip, even when everything was in order. And there was plenty of gossip about Gloria.

At first the girl said nothing about the carbuncle. But no child stands up during class, and Gloria did. When the teacher asked why, the girl hung her head, embarrassed. She was sent to the principal's office. Gloria wouldn't sit down—and wouldn't explain why. The principal sent her to the school nurse, who found that the girl had a carbuncle on her rear—one so bad that medical attention was necessary. So we—again Manuel would not go without me—took Gloria to a nearby charity hospital . . . and waited . . . and waited . . . and waited. Then took her back two more times.

"There's one bright side to this carbuncle business," Manuel said.

"I'd sure like to know what it is."

"I'll bet she's living a virtuous life with that thing on her stern."

When Gloria failed to return to school after the carbuncle was healed, we decided to tackle the courts. First Manuel located the girl's mother and induced her to sign a statement agreeing to transfer custody of Gloria to the juvenile probation court, asking that the girl be placed in a home. He had arranged for a Catholic home to take Gloria. Nothing much happened. Probation, knowing from years of experience that hundreds and hundreds of young Mexican-American girls turned to prostitution, since there were thousands upon thousands of young soldiers available as clients, saw little reason to concentrate on one girl. We simply could not get action on the case. School ended, Manuel left for good, and I took it for granted that I would not see Gloria again.

How wrong I was. She showed up the day school opened in September. Gloria was a pretty girl—large dark eyes, smooth light-brown skin, a neat hairdo, a blossoming figure that was definitely alluring, and a miniskirt that showed plenty of shapely legs.

The miniskirt revealed more than that—tatoo marks. And there were some on her arms. I flinched as I glanced at them, for memory brought back those tatoo marks on the Pachuco with the switchblade—and Gloria had been caught with a switchblade. Reaction at school was immediate. Gloria was sent home and told not to return until the tatoo marks were removed. Three days passed and no Gloria. So it was up to me, without any aid from Manuel this time, to carry on. I went to the grandmother's home.

Gloria was there. She said that only a doctor could remove the tatoo marks and there was no money to pay a doctor. A compromise occurred to me, and I went to a nearby home where there was a telephone (the grandmother had none) and called the principal. "Will you let Gloria come back if she covers the marks with bandaids until she can get them removed?" I asked.

"Why can't she get them off now?"

"It takes a doctor to do it and they have no money. I'll have to scout around and find some way of getting it done free."

He agreed and I took the girl back to school. Then I told the principal, "I'm going to file an attendance case against the grandmother if it's all right with you. I can't spend all my time re-trieving that girl and bringing her back here."

"Wouldn't it be better to just admit defeat?" the principal said. Occasionally we let a sixteen-year-old boy drop out if he had a job. On rare occasions a girl. But doing so tends to set a pattern.

"The girl is headed for a life of prostitution," I told the prin-cipal. "There is a chance, a tiny one, that she might be diverted into a better way of life—at least a way that most of us consider better."

"File if you want to," the principal said. "But isn't the mother the legal guardian?"

"Technically, I think so. But a judge might consider that the grandmother is the guardian. The girl is illegitimate and her mother turned her over to the grandmother when she was only a few weeks old. Gloria hardly knows her mother."

I filed and Gloria and her grandmother were hailed into justice of the peace court. "Where is the mother?" the J.P. asked.

"Judge, if you can find out I wish you'd let us know," a deputy constable answered, dropping some police mug shots of the mother on the judge's bench. "We want her on some charges."

The judge listened as Gloria and the grandmother told their story—and this time a professional interpreter translated for the grandmother, so we could be sure of what she said. Then I showed the judge my file. He agreed to turn the case over to juvenile probation with a recommendation that juvenile court take cus-tody and put the girl in a home.

We finally made it to juvenile court—still with no mother present. She had a way of vanishing into the night. And I think the judge, a Mexican-American, would have placed Gloria in the Catholic girls' home that had agreed to take her—except for a brilliant display of race prejudice in reverse.

The old grandmother, a rugged individual, showed up in court with an attorney. Not just an ordinary attorney—The Hawk.

He was a brilliant young Mexican-American lawyer and his name was Faustino Gavilan. Gavilan is the Spanish word for hawk, so, as other attorneys began getting the feel of his talons, they dubbed him The Hawk. The Hawk completely dismantled our case by creating the impression that we, a gang of Anglos, were deliberately persecuting the girl solely because she was Mexican-American.

If Manuel had been there, things might have been different. But Manuel wasn't there. The Hawk didn't humiliate me; he simply had all testimony that I might have given tossed out as hearsay. Manuel had handled the case. But the principal . . . seldom have I seen a man so completely shaken and humiliated on the witness stand. It was brutal, even though it was, in a way, fascinating—like a matador toying with a mighty bull before moving in for the kill.

Everything was wrong. The principal's records were not complete. And what kind of school did he run, warning the bus driver to keep a little girl near so he could watch her? A little Mexican-American girl. Did he do that to Anglo girls? Was this Anglo justice as we enforced it on Mexican-Americans in our schools? "You know the terrible effect such an order—banishing from the free world—will have on a sensitive child . . ."

I never could completely reconcile his line of questioning and browbeating with the facts at issue. Evidently the judge could— or was intimidated. For the judge, who had endured the same kind of race discrimination that The Hawk was talking about, dismissed our plea and gave the grandmother legal custody of Gloria.

The Hawk and I came face to face as I was leaving the courtroom. "Are you happy?" I asked.

"What do you mean?" he snapped.

"You've just condemned a fourteen-year-old girl to a life of prostitution. Congratulations." I walked on without waiting for an answer.

I didn't dream that Gloria would show up at school again. But there she was, tatoo marks still covered with bandaids. And soon she began to show in other ways—she was pregnant and it was becoming obvious. I took her to a doctor and had the pregnancy verified. She was dropped from the school rolls.

The baby was a girl. They named it Angelina [little angel] after its great-grandmother. The old woman had a new toy, a new plaything. She could start training little Angelina for a career of prostitution. And I heard that Gloria was getting along quite well as a prostitute, catering mainly to soldiers at the nearby military base.

I could never bring myself to feel any bitterness against that old grandmother—now great-grandmother. Life had been hard for her since her own childhood. Among the few bright moments were the joys of sex in earlier days—and, later, affection of the little ones. So she clung to them. They were the only human beings who needed her. And in trying to gain and hold their love, she enforced no discipline. The children went their merry way— into prostitution, which the old woman considered a pretty good way for a girl to get along in life.

In a way I admired her—maybe because she beat me down. I did, however, feel bitter toward The Hawk. Let him pick some other case in which to break Anglos for the humiliation they had caused him—some case in which the life pattern of a child was not at stake.

When the doctor verified Gloria's pregnancy, I called The Hawk and told him that Gloria was pregnant. He didn't believe me. So I had the pleasure of making a final thrust with the knife. "I have a doctor's certificate stating that she is pregnant," I said. "Would that be admissable in court or would you consider it hearsay?"

There was no answer.

White Invasion, 1: I Killed a Man

"We can't do a thing about her unless she commits a serious crime," the probation officer told Dwight, the graduate student I was supervising.

"Would it help if she went out and killed somebody?" Dwight asked.

"We go by the law, you go by your rules," the probation officer snapped.

And then Frances Jenkins, age fourteen, obliged by killing a man. But she didn't do it the right way or at the right place, so Probation still kept hands off. Frances was driving a man's car on a runaway trip to Louisiana, and she crashed into a bridge railing. The man was killed, Frances only shaken up. The Louisiana court agreed to release the girl to her father if he would come get her and take her away and guarantee that she never came back, which the father did. So Dwight and I renewed our campaign to do something for the girl before she moved permanently into the shadowy world of crime.

After she was brought back from Louisiana, Frances was morose and sullen, a bit withdrawn. This mood was in sharp contrast to her usual attitude of buoyant defiance. "I killed a man," she said, appearing to be genuinely sorry. Three weeks later she had a new boyfriend and was as lively and arrogant as ever—and out of school again.

There were six children in the Jenkins family, all marching single file down the road to delinquency. Since they were bunched close in age—not more than a two-year gap anywhere along the line—there were Jenkins kids all the way from the second grade to the ninth, last year of junior high.

As I began knowing them—and I know children only when they are in trouble—I could visualize seven more years of struggling with the Jenkins family. And I began making inquiries about openings at other school districts. Sure, one family can defeat a social worker if the family is large enough and lingers on forever. I soon concluded that my only hope for outlasting the Jenkins clan was to start whittling down from the top. Then I might be able to guide the younger ones along something resembling a normal life pattern. At the moment our major problem was Frances, although we weren't exactly having an easy time with Henry, oldest boy, and Larry, a year and a half younger than Henry.

This blond Anglo family from Chicago moved into a quiet, predominantly Mexican-American area in greater San Antonio. Perhaps it would be better to say they invaded the area. They reminded me of the Vandals who invaded the Mediterranean area fifteen hundred years ago—the Nordic Horde, as Dwight and I began calling them. They terrorized other families living near them and some not living near them. One family, after the parents came home and found Henry trying to choke their son to death, boarded up the house and fled as people flee an approaching hurricane. Other families were putting up "For Sale" signs, getting ready for flight.

The law tried. I mean *really* tried, as I learned from talking to a deputy constable and Probation people. But even though Henry was saying "I'm going to choke you to death" as he choked the smaller boy, there seemed to be nothing that the law could do. Henry argued that the boy lied about him. Chances are the boy told the truth—but to Henry the truth was a lie if it was not to his liking. One or more of the Jenkins horde would be held at the juvenile detention center for a couple of days, then back home they came, determined to set bigger and better records in terrorizing the community. Henry recruited followers and organized the first gang ever to operate in an elementary school in our district. It was new and exciting to those in the gang—terrifying to the fifth and sixth graders not in it.

Except for Larry, the Jenkins children were not mentally retarded. They were nice-looking blond kids, wore nice clothes that were always clean at the start of the school day, and were well mannered around adults most of the time. But they had a set of values entirely different from what we considered normal and legal. And their viciousness in destroying things, their cruelty in torturing and killing cats and dogs and chickens astonished me.

I will tell more about Henry and Larry in the next chapter. Now I want to tell the story of Frances, for it illustrates one of the major obstacles that must be hurdled in many cases if one is to help problem children—that is, the question of jurisdiction. Again and again the question of jurisdiction baffled Dwight and me as we tried to do something for the girl. Jurisdictional conflicts in labor unions seemed simple by comparison. Probation said the schools and Child Welfare should handle her . . . she was not a delinquent . . . had not committed a crime. Child Welfare said she was a delinquent and it was up to Probation. Or the schools. And school people were almost unanimous in their attitude—get *rid* of her. Why try to keep her? Let society at large worry about her.

You learn to cope with jurisdictional problems, even though they blossom in strange forms at times. There was the case of a boy who was an epileptic and was also mentally retarded. The state school for epileptics would not take him, because he was mentally retarded. The state school for the mentally retarded would not take him, because he was epileptic. How about cutting him in half?

At times I recall what I consider the classic jurisdictional case —a half-man, half-ape that was, supposedly, on the high seas headed for this country. It was a publicity stunt panned off on the newspapers by a wild-animal dealer, and his timing was perfect, for some Russian scientists were in Africa at the time, trying to produce a half-man, half-ape by artificially inseminating female chimps with sperm of human males. When the wild-animal dealer was finally cornered and asked to produce his "missing link" or admit that his story was phony, he gave newspapermen a really lovely explanation. Jurisdiction fouled things up, he said. Customs claimed jurisdiction over the ape part of the creature, immigration claimed jurisdiction over the human part. Since no agreement could be reached, customs and immigration took the creature back out to sea and threw it over the side.

Take Frances out to sea and throw her over the side.

I began getting clues in the delinquency pattern of the Jenkins children on my first visit to the home. I went there to find out why Frances was not in school. I was met at the door by a woman who said she was Mrs. Olsen, the housekeeper. No Mrs. Jenkins was mentioned, so I presumed that the mother was not part of the clan. "Have you known the family long?" I asked Mrs. Olsen.

"I knew them in Chicago," she said. "I was housekeeper for them there before their mother went off and left the children. I came here with them."

It became evident that she was more than a houseekeeper to Jenkins, less than a mother to the children, even though she tried. Resentment, particularly by the older children, toward her position in the home was a factor in the breakdown of discipline.

"I'm going to tell you the truth," Mrs. Olsen said, when I asked about Frances. "We don't know where that girl is. Her Daddy tries to keep her in her room. He locks the door. But she climbs out the window and goes off with a gang of kids, mostly boys. She's been gone for three days now."

"Has this happened before?"

"Sure, a lot of times. I don't have a bit of control over her or the older boys. And their father doesn't either. Now if they was my children . . ." She paused, embarrassed.

I learned that after the mother had abandoned the family, the father got a divorce. The judge urged him to put the children up for adoption. Jenkins said he wanted to keep his family together —with Mrs. Olsen's help he could take care of them.

Jenkins was a salesman and evidently a good one, judging by the nice home and good clothes the children had. He may have been competent at doing a selling job on strangers, but he sure didn't do much "selling" at home. He admitted, when we had a conference on my second visit to the home, that he had no control over Frances and little over the two older boys. Obviously he would have no control over the younger children in two or three years unless there was change. "The older ones never would pay any attention to Mrs. Olsen," he said. "Now they don't pay any attention to me."

I wondered why he and Mrs. Olsen did not get married, which might at least give her moral support in trying to "mother" the younger children. There was undoubtedly a good reason, but I ask few questions about the man-woman relationship in a home.

I did become convinced that in her escapades with boys, Frances was motivated in part by resentment against the situation at home.

"She's *not* my mother and has no business being there in *our* home," the girl said. "Why should I pay any attention to what she says?"

"But your own mother is not there and Mrs. Olsen is, trying to help the children," I reminded her.

"Trying to help, bah. She's the reason my mother left. And that youngest kid, Buddy, he's hers."

So Frances went her merry way, spending a night now and then with some boy, maybe several boys, in an abandoned home, spending a night occasionally with some man, maybe in a motel, and getting paid for her companionship. So what's wrong with becoming a prostitute? Maybe nothing. I am not arguing the question. But as long as Frances was in school, or supposed to be, she was my problem.

If the principal suspended her, which he could have done after three days' absence, I would probably be forced to file charges against the father. Not so good, as I knew from experience. The few cases I have filed were against parents who were deliberately flouting the compulsory attendance law. Jenkins was doing his best to conform—locking the door and so on.

I knew the youth who became Frances's lover soon after the accident in Louisiana. He was seventeen. When he was fifteen and in junior high, I had filed charges against his mother, a barmaid in a tavern. She was arrogant and abusive to us when we talked to her about keeping her son in school. Said the school people were "nosing into" her affairs.

Filing backfired on us. That woman came boiling into justice of the peace court with a lawyer in tow and proceeded to whip us down. Parents can do that in most truancy cases if they get a lawyer. The case begins to attract attention—gets in the newspapers. The justice of the peace, fearing that he will lose votes by seeming to persecute a "poor working woman struggling to support her boy" is not likely to fine the mother or slap her in jail. So the barmaid mother emerged triumphant. And we gave up. We made no further effort to keep her son in school.

The boy, Fred Albany, and Frances decided it would be fun to make a tour in his car, an old one that he had worked over. But Frances complained that she had no good clothes. She had seen the lovely clothes that Fred's mother had—saw them during her secret visits to the home with Fred when the mother was at work. How about taking some of those clothes? The mother would never miss them. Fred balked at stealing. But he finally agreed to tell Frances how she could get into the home without a key and left the rest to her. Ah, the lovely clothes. And the right size.

Frances made the same mistake that we at school had made—she underestimated that fiery barmaid. Evidently the barmaid had arranged with a neighbor to keep watch and call her. At any rate, she drove up in front of her home just as Frances was emerging laden with clothes. The clothes were worth far more than fifty dollars—a felony theft. If you want to get along in Texas by stealing, keep the value under fifty dollars. Crime is still measured in terms of cash.

Probation swung into action as though jabbed in the stern with a rusty needle. All that Probation-to-school-to-Child-Welfare-to-justice-of-the-peace-and-back-to-school nonsense came to a dead halt.

All Dwight and I knew about disposition of the case was rumor —at least for a time. And we were reluctant to call Probation, for relations in this particular case were a bit strained. We did know that Frances was no longer in school—and nobody suggested that I try to "retrieve" her and bring her back. So Dwight and I wondered. "Maybe they took her out to sea and threw her over the side," I suggested.

"What's that?"

"Nothing . . . just thinking of an old story. I sure hope they get the girl into a fairly good home and not condemn her to the state school. But it's out of my hands."

We did hear that Frances was being held, for the moment, at the juvenile detention center, called the Child Shelter.

Then I had to go to the Jenkins home to talk to Mrs. Olsen about Henry and Larry.

"Have you heard about Frances?" she asked. I hadn't.

"She's in that new Christian Faith Home," she said, and I could feel her sense of relief. "She's doing just fine there."

Maybe I should have felt a sense of victory, for I had urged Probation a dozen times to place the girl in a home before she was sent to the state school. But . . . jurisdiction . . . always jurisdiction . . . I still couldn't understand why the new Christian Faith Home had taken her after that theft . . . a felony. Dwight talked to Probation and got the story. "It's a brand new home for both boys and girls, and they were short on clientele," he said. "They took her to help fill out the list."

"What about the felony charge?"

"That was handled neatly," he said. "Do you know who was sitting in his car waiting for Frances when she came out with that bundle of clothes?"

"I can guess—Fred." Now I understood. The law had an ax hanging over mama's head. If she filed on Frances, the law would file on her son. She didn't file. So Probation got full cooperation from Jenkins in having Frances sent to the new Home.

A few weeks later I called the Home and talked to a social worker who had just been employed there. Frances was getting along fine. Other children liked her and she never missed a day at school—children from the Home were sent to a nearby public school. "If we can just keep her here until she's seventeen, our age limit, she might made a good adjustment in life."

A brilliant idea suddenly came to me. "Has the Home filled its quota?" I asked.

"I talked to the director this morning, and he said we could handle a few more," the social worker said.

"Thanks."

Then I explained my "brilliant" plan to Dwight and we launched our campaign. If the Christian Faith Home needed more children, we had them—Henry and Larry. "Let's move the whole family out there," I suggested.

"Charge!" Dwight said.

White Invasion, 2: The Blowtorch Kids

There is no tide in the water of a swimming pool. But this particular swimming pool was a key factor in turning the life tide for Henry and Larry Jenkins—at least temporarily. I do no speculating on their future. Henry was second in line among the six Jenkins children—the Nordic Horde. As I have mentioned, Frances, first in line, had been placed in the new Christian Faith Home for children.

"Are you happy at home?" I asked Henry after Frances was placed in the Home.

"With that woman there?" he said scornfully. "Of course not. I hate her. I hate everything in the house."

"That woman" was Mrs. Olsen, housekeeper . . . plus . . .

"How would you like to move to the new Christian Faith Home where Frances is?" I asked. "You and Larry both. It would be a little like getting the family back together."

"Say, I was out there Sunday seeing Frances. You know what they got there?"

"Tell me."

"They got a swimming pool as big as a football field. Finest I ever saw in my life. If I went there I could swim in the pool all summer."

Quite a nice alternative to "swimming" in the state correctional school for a few years, and there wasn't much doubt about that . . . especially if Henry and Larry were permitted to roam the streets after school ended.

"I think I can arrange it so you will be able to swim in that pool all summer," I told him. "I'll start right away trying to get you and Larry in the Home as soon as school is over."

"Well . . . I . . . I'm not so sure about going there for good," he hedged. "If I go there I can't get out and do anything, can I?" To Henry getting out and doing things included such delicate activities as setting fire to a dog after pouring lighter fluid on it or stealing a bicycle or deliberately vandalizing a home. No, he wouldn't be able to do that sort of thing. But I made no issue of it at the time, preferring to dwell on the fine life that he and Larry would have during the summer.

"You'd like it," I assured him. "You'll have Frances and Larry there with you. And they've got a lot more than the swimming pool—games and outings and a fine library. Mrs. Elliot and I can arrange for you to carry on your library work. She says you're doing fine at it." I had to build on one of the few noncriminal urges that I had observed in Henry—his love for work in the library. And Mrs. Elliot did say that he was doing unusually well. It was easy to steer him into library work, for Frances had done some work there. And Mrs. Elliot always came to my rescue when work in the library served to give some child direction—an incentive.

I knew that deputy constables, deputy sheriffs, police and probation officers were closing in on the boys, and the result was predictable—confinement in the state correctional school, probably followed by the "graduate school," the state penitentiary. But catching the boys wasn't easy. Henry was a truly clever boy. He had an IQ of 125, "college material," as the saying goes. Getting the consent of Henry and Jenkins would be sufficient. Larry would be no problem—he trotted along obediently behind Henry, doing what Henry said.

"Mrs. Elliot says I do fine in the library?" Henry asked, quite pleased.

"She says you could go on to college and maybe make a career of library work—maybe become director of some library." Put the glory paint on. And I wasn't deceiving the boy. Henry was impressed. He would go.

I called the director of the Home. He said to have Jenkins send in an application, along with the school records of the two boys. He seemed quite optimistic. Dwight went to work on the details. "You won't be here in September, but I will," I told him. "But unless we can whittle that Nordic Horde down from the top, I'm not sure how long I can stay."

"Trust me," Dwight said, and he got together the necessary— so we thought—papers and records and took them to the director of the Home. We waited, serenely at first, then nervously after the newspapers came out with a big headline about the "Blowtorch Kids."

Maybe Henry and Larry didn't do it. But the police thought they did and the principal thought they did and Probation thought they did. So did Dwight and I. And I was afraid the people at the Christian Faith Home might hear enough rumors to make some kind of connection, even if no charges were filed against the boys.

At least the Home was dormant insofar as applications for the entry of Henry and Larry were concerned. The Home had readily accepted Frances because it was short of material and she was a pretty, bright girl with no criminal record. But the list was almost full now, I learned, and in the lingo of Texas cedar choppers, people running the Home could afford to be choicy. I called and checked. And from that moment until the close of school, two months later, I received a liberal education about certain techniques and procedures in children's homes. The technique in this case was immobility.

Most people are slaves to time when it is of no consequence. Invention of the watch was probably the greatest catastrophe to mankind between invention of the plow and invention of the atom bomb. But when time is vital, when the destiny of a child is at stake, time may stand still. Time stood still as Ramon rode the borrowed bicycle to his death. If I had had a few more days. . .

I thought Henry and Larry were the Blowtorch Kids because the break-in and vandalism fit their pattern of operation. At the junior high, which Henry was attending at the time, all the expensive electric typewriters and calculating machines and other valuable equipment were locked in a vault every afternoon. The door was solid steel, like the door of a bank vault. Someone had cut a rectangular hole in the door by using a blowtorch. Then that someone, or his smaller accomplice, had gone inside and wielded a hammer, smashing all those valuable machines. Nothing was stolen . . . pure vandalism.

The Nordic Horde. Who else? No adult could have squeezed through the little hole cut in the door. Only a child could have entered. So the finger pointed to Henry and Larry. And for good reason. They were suspected but never caught in similar incidents. They would break into a home when the occupants were away and smash things they decided not to steal. They were highly selective in stealing—careful to take nothing that might lead back to them. Bear in mind that 125 IQ of Henry. They stole bicycles. At least the law officers thought they did. Any time a bicycle was stolen, the law headed for the Jenkins home. Sometimes officers found the stolen bicycle—invariably it was too far from the Jenkins home to constitute a solid case against the boys.

The blowtorch incident fit still another pattern—the manner in which the boys, particularly Henry, used fire. "Henry caught a chicken and wanted to pour lighter fluid on it and set fire to it," another delinquent, member of a new gang that Henry formed when he was advanced to junior high, told me. "But he was out of lighter fluid, so he broke the chicken's neck and threw it on the roof."

"What roof?" I asked.

"This one," the boy said, pointing upward. "The chicken is up there now."

"Why was Henry out of lighter fluid?"

"He used it all up on a dog and set fire to it," the boy said. "It sure did run and howl."

Larry, who showed indications of minimal brain damage, was equally sadistic although not as resourceful. One morning when I arrived at school I found his classroom teacher in a state of near panic. "That fiendish little monster—that Larry—was throwing a little white kitten against the brick wall of the building when I got here," she said. "Its little pink nose was all bloody. Then the fiend stuffed it in a paper sack and was trying to smother it when I got to him. The kitten died anyway, from being thrown against the wall. I can't stand the sight of him any longer!"

I told her I would see if I could get Larry transferred, and I managed to do so. But the overall problem remained unsolved. These boys, the Blowtorch Kids, were not going to fit into the school pattern. On that point there was no doubt.

I turned to the Christian Faith Home, begging for salvation. And encountered the immovable object, as I have so many times in my work. I could see that May 30 deadline rushing at me, so I called the Home again and talked to Mrs. Benton, the newly employed social worker.

"We have only the father's application and part of the school record," she said blandly. "We need complete school records, all the way back the line, and many other records." She ran through the list. It was monumental. And in view of the manner in which Jenkins dragged his feet when action was vital, hope seemed small.

Dwight began devoting practically all his time to the Nordic Horde. "I figure that since I'm a Nordic, I owe you an obligation to get this albatross off your neck," he said, smiling.

We got unexpected help from Jenkins. When I told Mrs. Olsen about our plans, she went wild with joy and immediately started putting pressure on Jenkins, something she had never done in the past. And the boys began prodding their father, mainly because Dwight and I were putting heat on them. I never said so directly, but I did let them know in a roundabout way that the *real* Blowtorch Kids were headed for a life in prison . . . unless . . .

Finally all the records—birth certificates, doctors' reports, psychologists' reports, school records from way back the line and so on—were duly delivered to the Home. And I personally delivered a letter from Mrs. Elliot, our school librarian, in which she said that Henry showed unusual ability in library work and might, if given a chance, build a career in the field. I think a really nice place in Heaven should be reserved for school librarians. They have been tops on the list of those who have helped me with problem children—maybe because librarians continue to read and learn . . . and grow.

In dealing with people at the Home I leaned heavily on Henry's high IQ while saying little about that of Larry. I had learned that these homes that send their children to public schools tend to screen out the low-IQ children—the ones most desperately in need of help—and pick those who are brighter, mainly for prestige purposes. They do not want public school people saying, "That place with all those dumb kids in it."

I waited. No call. May 30 was zipping at me. Finally I called the social worker at Child Shelter, the juvenile retention center. "What's the best way to get action from the Christian Faith Home?" I asked.

"Nag the director," she said. "He's a nice guy but he drags his feet. Now he's got that social worker out there mainly to screen children . . . to pick only those who will reflect credit on the Home. But nag him . . . it works."

I nagged, then nagged more. Then Henry informed me that he had decided not to go to the Home. He wanted to be free. Henry was almost thirteen, and his character pretty well formed. I knew that—and I decided some shock therapy might be in order. "How would you like to be locked up in the state reform school and moved from there to the state penitentiary?" I asked.

"But . . . how can they . . . I'm not . . ."

"You're not what?" I cut in. "The police know more about you and Larry than you think. I'd sure hate to see you shipped off and locked up, but if you turn down the chance to go to this Home . . ."

He was a smart kid. He knew from what I said that some very unpleasant things were going to happen to him . . . unless. He knuckled under and said he would go to the Home.

I called the social worker at the Home. And ran smack into another road block. It was obvious to me by then that she had somehow made a connection between the boys and the blowtorch incident . . . and that she was not going to let them in the Home unless I forced the issue. "We are wondering if it wouldn't be wise to have custody of the boys placed in juvenile court," she said serenely. "Experience has shown that things don't always work out so well when parents retain custody and can drop by at any time and take their children out."

"What experience are you speaking of?" I asked. "Your own?" I had checked and knew that this was her first job with a children's home.

"Well, that's what the records indicate," she said.

"The father isn't going to go there and get any child out," I told her. "It was a monumental task getting him to help with those records. And juvenile courts do not operate as they once did. They can't just take custody and send a child to a home unless there is agreement all around. That's been battled out in higher courts." I didn't add that juvenile court could take custody if the youngster committed a serious crime—Blowtorch Kids.

She promised to talk to the director. Delay . . . delay. I called the director myself. Nag . . . nag . . . nag. He reassured me. They would take Henry and Larry. But he wanted harmony in his staff, so would I please handle details through the social worker, who had been employed to deal with such matters. Round and round we go—on the way to the state correctional school—then on to that graduate school, the state penitentiary.

I called the social worker again the next day, which was the last day of school. Henry was in my office . . . he had come to tell me goodbye before going to the Home—he thought. He had come to thank me. His blue eyes brightened at the prospect of diving into that king-size swimming pool . . . of being a librarian. I think the boy was beginning to realize that it was time for him to move along certain life patterns other than vandalism.

"The matter was to be considered at a staff conference," the social worker told me. "Some of the people here think the boys might fit better into our branch home at Waco."

"But that's two hundred miles away and this is the last day of school and if . . ." I stopped talking and hung up. Then I called the director. Nag, nag. "Henry is here in my office," I said. "He and Larry are ready to come. Your social worker says a staff conference is necessary."

He mumbled a hmmm . . .

"May I send the father and the boys there so your staff can see them and talk to them?" I asked. "After all, you have given me, and I have given the boys, every reason in the world to believe that you will accept them . . ."

The director agreed.

I called Jenkins at his place of work. I moved that immovable object by telling him that unless he came to school and got the boys and took them to the Home immediately the end was in sight for them, and I could no longer help. When Jenkins showed up I set off with Henry in my car, asking Jenkins to follow me to the elementary school that Larry attended. I led Larry out to his father's car, and the three of them took off . . . "hunting for a home," like that boll weevil in the old song that Leadbelly sang.

I called Mrs. Olsen the following morning. When she recognized my voice she shouted, "They're gone!" She said the people at the Home had called earlier that morning and told Jenkins to bring the boys. "Mr. Jenkins just left with them a few minutes ago," she said.

So the Nordic Horde was whittled down to three, the oldest, Bobby, in fourth grade. I would be watching him when school reopened in September. I would move in at the least hint of trouble. I was determined to stop that march down the trail to delinquency.

A week before the Christmas holidays I called the social worker at the Christian Faith Home and asked about the Jenkins children. They were doing fine, she said. Henry was surprisingly capable in library work. And Frances had adjusted nicely. Larry wasn't overly bright, which I knew quite well, but he was getting along. No trouble.

I went to the library and relayed the information to Mrs. Elliot. "You know what I think?" I said. "I think the school faculty should be made up entirely of librarians. Maybe it's because you people keep on learning—and growing. Anyway, thanks for helping me through one of the toughest situations I've ever faced."

"Maybe we'd have a better world if more people faced such tough situations instead of taking the easy way out," Mrs. Elliot said.

Come on In, Coach

As Big Bill Tilden, the principal, and I stepped onto the front porch of the little frame house, he hesitated and said, "Something in there stinks. I can smell it out here."

"I told you the cut on little Al's foot had become infected," I said. "But you wanted to be sure he wasn't playing hooky, so let's go in and see."

The principal didn't move as I walked toward the door.

"Come on in, coach," I urged. "Let's take a look."

The principal had been advanced, if it could be considered that, from coach of the junior high football team to principal of an elementary school. Those of us who knew him during his coaching years still called him "coach." It pleased him.

"I can't go in there," the big, husky man said. "I'm beginning to feel upset at my stomach . . . that stink . . . it's sickening to a man with a weak stomach." Coaches with weak stomachs aren't as rare as one might think. Victory or ulcers . . . maybe victory and ulcers.

There was an old mesquite tree in the yard not far from the house, and one branch extended parallel to the ground. The coach-turned-principal wobbled to the branch and reached up and grasped it. His body sort of sagged. I thought he was going to vomit.

"Come on in, coach," I urged again. "We should check out this situation. That's what you came here to do."

"I can't," he muttered weakly. "You go in if you want to. I'll take your word for it."

"But you told me one of your football players wouldn't pay any attention to a little scratch—you said Al was just goofing off."

The principal said nothing. He was pretty sick.

I knocked on the door and Al's mother let me in. We had met before. I asked about Al. Real sick, she said—high fever. I had barely detected the offensive odor outside the home. The coach-principal sure had sensitive smelling equipment. Inside the home the stench was overpowering, and it got worse as I neared the bed where the eight-year-old boy was lying. "You'll have to get him to the clinic right away," I said. "He might have gangrene."

"I don't have any way to get there," the mother said. "My husband has the truck out at the spinach farm where he works."

I didn't have to ask if she had money for a taxi. Stoop laborers in South Texas, or anyplace else in the nation, do not ride in cabs, and the Espinoza family was no exception. "I'll take him," I said. "Let's go—right now."

The name Al is a short, Anglicized version of the boy's real name, Alfredo. Part of a trend in the Mexican-American part of the nation—until the rise of the Chicano. Enrique became

Henry, Ricardo was Richard, and so on. Not any more. Chicanos are now proud of their Spanish names, part of their declaration of independence, new style.

Mrs. Espinoza and I carried the frail little boy out of the house, and, as we emerged, the coach-principal turned pale and moved his head so he could not see us. There was no way he could avoid getting a strong whiff of the decaying flesh—Strange Fruit.

"This boy is real sick," I called to Big Bill. "I'm taking him to the clinic, then they'll move him on to the hospital. Come help us."

He just shook his head . . . no.

For three months Big Bill Tilden, as he was called during his coaching days, had been needling me to "get those hooky players back in school and keep them there." The name *Big Bill Tilden* wasn't working wonders, as the superintendent and the school board had thought it would when they made him principal. I have no idea why they assumed the name would suddenly bring all the wayward boys back to school; the original Big Bill Tilden, famous tennis player of a half century ago, had no meaning to these kids, especially the Chicanos. In fact, there wasn't even a tennis court at the elementary school. But . . . "Send me in, coach."

Big Bill didn't send them in, because they weren't there. Instead of going up, ADA (average daily attendance) began sagging. I could picture Big Bill kneeling beside his bed at night, praying, "Oh Lord, *please* let my ADA go up just a few points, will you?"

He got no answer. So the superintendent, noting the sag, began putting pressure on Big Bill, and Big Bill transferred it to me. I was letting the kids hoodwink me . . . and on and on. I got fed up with it and told Big Bill, "Okay, I'll show you why some of the kids aren't in school. You come along with me and we will do some home visiting."

"It's a deal," he said, confident that the magic of his domineering ways would start a flood of kids back to school. The home is not the football field—so there was Big Bill, the 250-pound clinging vine—on the verge of vomiting.

"I'll come back and get you," I said.

And I said to myself, "It ain't so easy, is it Isadore?"

"What did you say?" Mrs. Espinoza asked.

"Just talking to myself and enjoying every word of it," I told her.

Joe Bernstein, first violin—or concertmaster, as you choose to term it—of the Houston Symphony Orchestra, was a friend of ours when my husband and I lived in Houston. Joe complained occasionally about Isadore, second violin. "He warts me all the time," Joe said, "especially when I'm negotiating a difficult passage. I'll get him some day." And Joe did.

The conductor was ill during one concert and Joe took over. He moved Isadore up to first violin, then selected a symphony in which the part of the first violin is fiendishly complex.

"I can't play that," Isadore said, visibly shaken.

"You *will* play it," Joe said.

Isadore did. The first violin is not far from the conductor, and, as Isadore was struggling and sweating, Joe would lean slightly toward him and say, in a low voice, "It ain't so easy, is it Isadore?" Isadore struggled harder and sweat more.

Smiling all the time, for the benefit of the audience, Joe would say, barely loud enough for Isadore and a few others in the string section to hear, "Play, Isadore . . . swine!" More struggling. More sweating. Isadore lacked Joe's remarkable technique and beautiful tone. Play, Isadore . . . swine.

As I drove away, leaving the heavyweight clinging to the branch, I couldn't avoid muttering, "It ain't so easy, is it Isadore?"

I don't care whether a principal has been a coach or a band director or a cafeteria manager, as long as he is moderately intelligent, competent, and humane in his dealings with teachers and children. But experience has taught me to move with caution any time I get a principal who has been a coach or a band director. And the number is astonishing—entirely out of proportion to the total number of qualified persons.

The coach and the band director are in position to win friends —the right kind—and influence people. They do that. A coach puts a kid who can't play worth a hoot on the squad—if the kid's father is on the school board. A band director takes in a tone-deaf kid (he can always bang on a drum) if the boy's father is an influential civic leader. And plenty of public exposure for coach and band director—none for teachers. So up the rope they go— and people like me, along with many children, take the rap.

It usually takes a coach two or three years to learn (if he ever does) that you can't whip the general run of children into line after the manner of an army sergeant whipping recruits into line. The coach concentrates his interest, when he becomes principal, almost entirely on the kind of "clean-cut" boy who is a football prospect. The band director usually has little patience with children who know nothing about music and can't learn. There is no balance—no recognition of the wide variation in attitudes and conduct and capacities of children in varied areas of human endeavor.

So I have had some mighty battles with coach-principals, and a few with band director–principals. And by the time Big Bill showed up and began tossing his weight at me, I was ready.

When I returned to the Espinoza home after the school nurse had rushed Al to the hospital, Big Bill was sitting beside the road, plenty far from the home in order to avoid the polluted air. He eased his bulk into the car and I started driving. "How is the boy?" he asked.

"Pretty bad shape. They rushed him to the hospital. He may

lose the leg—playing hooky isn't a good idea, is it?" Play Isadore, swine!

"I'm sure sorry," he said. "And I'm ashamed for not being able to help you. I just couldn't."

"Thousands of little children can't always do the things we demand of them," I said.

"I understand . . . I get your point." He noticed little huts along the unpaved street and said, slightly alarmed, "Where are we going?"

"We've just started our tour," I said. "Got seven homes on my list. Next is Benny Price. His father is an alcoholic . . . broke the boy's arm beating him. The mother kicked the father out and turned to prostitution . . ."

"I'll take your word for it," Big Bill said. "We don't have to go there."

"Then those three little children with sore eyes and lice . . ."

"Stop!" he said. "I'm feeling sick again."

As long as your opponent in the boxing ring is still on his feet, flatten him. Do no meditating on the quality of mercy when dealing with people who show none. "And that wheelchair mother . . . so crippled with arthritis that . . ."

"For God's sake stop!" Bill shouted. I stopped the car.

"You said they were playing hooky," I reminded him. "You've been giving me a rough time . . ." Play, Isadore.

"I'll take your word for it from now on," he said. "For everything. Just drive me back to school. You might spring a leper on me next." He managed a weak smile.

"We had a child with leprosy in Houston . . . a case I was working on . . ." I decided to quit. Actually Big Bill wasn't a bad guy. But his formula for discipline, as demonstrated on the football field, simply did not fit into the general school pattern. And he struggled to make it fit.

That smell of rotting flesh deeply moved him. And I began explaining, in a quiet way, the nature of problems confronting me.

I guess I lectured him all the way back to school—he listened with all three ears. "I work with the ones you wouldn't give a second look on the football field," I said. "The small, the sickly, the withdrawn, the frightened. But they're people, just as the all-American boy is. And they're my problem, although they should be the problem of the whole school organization. These little kids, most of them unwanted, must be given a second look . . . a second and third and fourth chance if necessary . . ."

I got through to him. "You'll have complete cooperation from me all the rest of the way," he said, as we drove up to the school building.

He was as good as his word. Even better than I expected. During the remaining two years that Big Bill and I worked together, I was able to mark "Closed with success" on many files—more than in other schools. I could do that because I had Big Bill's solid backing. And, thank you Lord, his ADA went up.

An incident in the cafeteria not long before I left the school was indicative of the deep impact that the Al Espinoza case had made on Big Bill. He and I and a couple of teachers were having lunch together, and I noticed that he carefully pushed the spinach off his plate onto a saucer. He used a paper napkin to make the transfer . . . didn't want to touch the stuff with his knife or fork.

"I thought you made your athletes eat spinach to get a lot of iron," I said.

"How do I know Al's father didn't pick that stuff?" he said. "That gangrene . . ."

"But the boy got well and that was almost two years ago," I reminded him.

"I just don't have any craving for spinach," Big Bill said, and we exchanged friendly smiles.

Know what? I haven't been able to eat spinach since that day.

The Cat House

It wasn't *that* kind of cat house. It was a neat little white house with a flat green roof built especially for the four-legged kind of cat. In this case, a kitten named Fearless Fosdick.

We named him that because he was afraid of everything. Since no sun shone inside the little house that Danny had built for him, Fearless wouldn't enter it. Probably afraid a mouse would attack him. But he did spend many luxurious hours stretched out on the roof of the house, letting the sunshine bathe his body. And the combination of kitten and house and friendship with two understanding adults helped the disturbed little boy toward a more pleasant way of life.

In handling the case I violated one basic rule of my work procedure. I let one of my problem children come to our home. It would be more accurate to say that he came without permission or warning. After that I couldn't or wouldn't stop him.

What do you do when a lonely child who can't read and has difficulty talking stands at your door with a box of candy on which is printed "Be My Valentine?" You ask him in. Then you get him a coke and insist that he eat some of the candy. And next time he is standing at the door with a furry little kitten. Then he shows up with a house for the kitten, and away we go, with no end in sight.

Danny was in the process of adopting my husband and me, and neither of us was tough enough to stop him. Every time I steeled myself to tell him, that drawing of his would flash before my eyes. The deserted street, the car, the crumpled bicycle, and the dead body of a little boy. At the bottom was printed, "I wish I was dead. Everybody hates me. Here is a picture of me dead."

Mrs. Cunningham, the classroom teacher, had asked each child to draw a picture of himself. She was shocked by Danny's drawing. So was I. It reminded me of some of the "self-portraits" drawn by black children—no face.

"I feel terrible about it," the teacher said when she came to my office for help. "I feel so guilty letting that little fellow just sit there. He can't read, so he can't learn anything from books. He even has trouble talking—the other children make fun of him. And I just let him sit there alone with his misery."

"I encounter that 'everyone hates me' attitude quite often," I consoled. "I never take it lightly, but most of the time it is temporary and can be changed."

"What can we do?" the teacher asked.

"Let me spend a half-hour a week with him, and I will arrange for our speech therapist to do the same. I'll work on his reading and writing while she works on his speech. And maybe I can find out the things that are disturbing him in other areas."

Danny started his weekly half-hour conferences with me, and

soon he was enjoying them. This was something new to him, adults showing an interest in him and trying to help. He began liking the conferences so much that he asked where I lived. Without any thought of consequences, I told him.

"Why that's right close to where I live," he said.

I thought no more about it until he knocked gently at our door. It was "Be My Valentine." Then Fearless Fosdick. Then the cat house. Then . . . "One way or another, we've got to slow him down," my husband said. "He left only a few minutes ago. This time he brought reinforcements—a little pal. Are you going to turn our place into a home for your problem children?"

"I'll think of something," I said.

"I like the kid and don't want to hurt him," my husband continued. "But he breaks in on my work at times . . ."

"I know."

Danny was the middle child in a family of three children. The family came to our city from Dallas during the summer, and Danny was put in the fifth grade, mainly because of his age and size. Soon he was demoted to the fourth grade. "He can't do fourth grade work any better than he could fifth grade," Mrs. Cunningham said. "I doubt if he could pass in second grade. He can't read. And listen to the way he talks."

The story Danny began unfolding to me at our first conference was one I have heard hundreds of times. Everybody hates me, other boys throw rocks at me, the teacher doesn't like me. The same pattern—with two exceptions. Danny couldn't read. And he had difficulty talking.

His older brother had dropped out of school and departed, a measure of relief for Danny, who said the brother loved to "beat on me." The boy's sister, four years younger, warted him, he said. His father either ignored him or gave him a rap on the head. His mother was always complaining. So he was lonely.

What child wouldn't be in such a situation? And he couldn't break out of the trap as many boys can, because of his speech difficulty.

The speech therapist and I thought he had MBI (minimal brain injury) and that it was in the part of the brain that controls speech. The word *mother* came out *muddl*. *Brother* sounded still stranger, something like *bwuddl*. He had a rugged time with the letter *r*, especially when it started a word. And this difficulty was not environmentally acquired, as I realized in talking to other members of the family. Not comparable to the *yeah* instead of *year* in the speech of the late President Kennedy, as he clearly demonstrated by saying *Cuber* instead of *Cuba*.

I asked the mother about possible brain damage. She told me a long story about taking her boy from doctor to doctor in Dallas, spending so much time at the chore that she lost her job. "They gave him all them tests," she said, "and said there was nothing wrong with his brain. He's just not smart—like his Daddy. His Daddy is a fine mechanic, one of the best. But you put a book in front of him . . ."

"Maybe Danny will become a fine mechanic like his father," I suggested.

"It sure looks that way. I bet he's taken that bike of his apart and put it back together a hundred times just to be doing it."

That gave me an idea. But first there was the business of reading. I had several first-grade books in my office, and on Danny's next visit I got one out. He was embarrassed. "Those books are for the first grade," he said.

"I won't let anybody see them," I told him. "They're just for you and me."

I would hold the "little book," as Danny called it, in position where both of us could see a page, then I would read—very slowly. Then Danny would read, still slower.

He had to master those little books before he could move on to

what he considered big books. Once he realized that I was paying no attention to his strange manner of pronouncing words, he
began to gain confidence. I think that's one thing that had
blocked his reading progress, especially in class. If he read out
loud, other children, and maybe even the teacher, would laugh.
Ridicule. So he developed what might be considered a reading
complex . . . book phobia. I "uncomplexed" this situation, although it took many weeks of doing . . . and plenty of help from
the speech therapist, even though he wasn't changing his pro-
nunciation much, mainly his attitude toward it.

Then I took Danny to Miss Elliot, the librarian, and said he
wanted some "bigger books," as he termed anything at third-
grade level or above. I nodded to the librarian and she understood. So we got bigger books and went to work on them. And
all that time I was teaching Danny to write—or print, which was
the way he made letters.

One day he was quite excited when he came in for our conference. "I can read every sign between here and home," he said.

"Wonderful."

"And I've been riding my bike all around and I can read all
the signs." Of course he didn't say *read*—it sounded closer to
weed. Who cared? He didn't say *Cuber*.

Well, I decided it was time to put that idea of mine to the test
—it was time to give Danny some public display.

"Your mother says you are good at doing things with your
hands," I told him.

"I'm pwutty good," he admitted.

"Well, they're going to have an arts and crafts fair here at the
school. How about making something and entering it?"

At first he was reluctant. Instantly he thought that he might
be called on to talk before many people. And regardless of what
the mother said about all those brain tests by specialists in Dallas,

I still believed that Danny had minimal brain injury in the area that controls speech—possibly due to insufficient oxygen at birth. But there was definitely no handicap in the use of his hands, so I persuaded him to make something and enter it in the fair.

He made a lovely miniature house and inside it he rigged a tiny blink-on, blink-off light. It charmed the children, and Danny stood by gloating as they praised it. And he won first prize—a blue ribbon and a "big book." More cause for pride.

The next day another victory. Danny came breezing into my office holding a paper. He wouldn't let me see it—he read it to me. Wanted to show that he could read. It was a certificate from the librarian saying that Danny Green had read the required number of books for a special reading award. "I'm going to show this to Daddy and prove to him that I'm not a dummy, like he says I am," Danny said. Fine way to help a son who has a handicap that can, if not handled carefully, wreck his life—calling him a dummy.

I urged Danny to enter his little house in the district arts and crafts fair for elementary schools of the whole school system. He did. And again he won first prize and a whole set of "big books." Then came the incident of the cat and the cat house.

Danny already considered himself a welcome visitor at our home because of the "Be My Valentine" incident. At one of our conferences he said, "Would you like to have a little kitten?"

I was caught without warning. And in dealing with disturbed children I try to follow a rule of never saying "no," unless I am forced to, which is seldom. These kids have heard enough no's from others. "I've always wanted a furry little kitten, but . . ." I started.

"We've got five cute little kittens at our home," Danny cut in. "You want a boy kitten or a girl kitten?"

"Wait a minute, Danny. My husband . . ."

"They're real cute," he continued, with growing enthusiasm. Obviously he wanted to do something for me in return for what I had done for him. "The little kitty won't bother your husband. He'll like it."

I was weakening and he knew it. It's wrong to deny a child, a handicapped child, the privilege of doing something for you in return. You make his little gesture seem puny. I knew my husband's attitude—no pets. I also knew that if a kitten was there ... fait accompli... "I'll take a chance," I said.

Danny arrived at our apartment before I did. When my husband answered the knock on the door, there stood Danny, holding the kitten. "You'll have to talk to my wife about that kitten," my husband said.

"I already have," Danny said triumphantly. "She's out getting him a box and some food." So into the house went Danny boy plus the kitten ... and the looks my husband gave me when I arrived with a box and some food and cat litter...

Fearless Fosdick settled serenely into his new environment. But in Danny's opinion, one thing was missing. Fearless should have a little house of his own, out in the small patio in front of our apartment. The boy showed up a week later pushing a wheelbarrow in which there was a neat little cat house.

Now Danny had a legitimate reason to call at our home. Fearless was, in way, a relative. And when I told him that Fearless wouldn't go into the little house, probably because it was so dark, Danny came up with a neat solution to the problem. He brought that blink-on, blink-off light he had used to win the arts and crafts prizes and installed it in the cat house. Fearless loved it. He would get inside and stare at the blinking light. A cat is a dopey creature about a bright electric light. Turn one on when the cat is facing it, maybe only a few feet away, and the stupid creature seems never to consider turning his head. He just stares

at the light—maybe goes to sleep facing it. Danny was so pleased
with his gift to us that he wanted to spend a night in the cat house
with Fearless, but it was too small.

Things were moving nicely for the boy who had been so isolated and wretched. He was completely overcoming his book
phobia, and he could write (or print) fairly well. "I'm going to
pass him to the fifth grade unless the principal objects, and I'm
pretty sure he won't," Mrs Cunningham said. "It would be a
mistake to keep him here another year. He's already two years
behind and bigger than the other children."

When the school year ended, Danny became a more frequent
visitor at our home, and much of the time he brought a smaller
boy, a new pal, with him. His excuse for coming was always the
same—to see Fearless, his protégé.

Fearless was growing fast and beginning to explore the big
patio of the apartment complex. His efforts to win friends and
influence cats didn't work out the way Mr. Carnegie said they
should. He came home now and then with scratches across his
face and fang holes in his tail. We mentioned that to Danny, and
he said, "What if he gets married and brings his wife here to have
her kittens?"

"Tomcats don't get married and bring their wives home," my
husband said. "All they get is visiting privileges, and they have
to battle for those."

Danny was puzzled for a moment, then he broke out in a big
laugh when he understood. After he left, my husband said, "I'm
nearing the end of this road. We've got to slow that kid down."

"I know," I admitted.

"I don't want to hurt him any more than you do. I've watched
you work on this case, and I think you've come near to perform-
ing a miracle. But when I hear that soft, sort of pleading knock
on the door..."

"I'll handle it," I said. "He's my problem child, not yours. He was so lonely and wretched and walled off . . . practically no human contacts . . . just ridicule and scorn . . ."

"I'm not suggesting we cut the kid off," my husband cut in. "Just slow him down a little."

"I'll work it out."

A few weeks later there was a knock at the door, and I noticed my husband flinch. The same soft, pleading knock. It was Danny, and I braced myself for the inevitable. But it was a despondent little boy who stood there at the door. "We're moving away, and I won't see you and your husband and Fearless any more," he said.

"Are you moving out of town?"

"No, but we're moving way across town."

"You can ride your bike across town and see Fearless and us," I said. I got no reproving look from my husband. He knew, just as I did, that Danny would make that long trip only a few times.

He came twice. On the last visit he looked in vain for Fearless. "The other tomcats around here are bigger and they were about to kill him," I said. "We had him at the vet's four times. Then some friends who live out in the country gave him a home, where he can hunt mice and not be chewed up by other tomcats."

Then Danny told us his own good news. "I'm working," he said. "My Daddy lets me work as his helper in the garage. I'm going to be a mechanic, like he is. He says I'm learning fine."

"That's just great," I told him. "You can do wonderful things with your hands."

He beamed. Then he glanced at our little patio and noticed the empty cat house, with no light blinking. We had disconnected it. "Say, if you want a furry little kitten . . . a little girl kitten . . ."

"No more cats," my husband cut in. He doesn't dislike pets per se. The big problem is that he flatly refuses to have any neutered pets around. And so it's up to us to more or less supervise the sex life of any pet we have. Supervision isn't always easy, as proved by the Fearless Era.

We didn't see Danny again. But it wasn't lonely around our place very long. We now have a lady cat named Mona Lisa—the look on her face is as inscrutable as that on the face of Leonardo's lady. And our Mona Lisa has reason for that look—she is about to present us with grandchildren. We hooked up the blink-on, blink-off light in the house that Danny built, and Mona Lisa loves it.

If you wonder how Mona Lisa happens to be a member of our family despite my husband's flat "No more pets," listen and I will explain. She "speaks" only Spanish. We got her on a trip to the Rio Grande. And my husband has a soft spot for Chicanos. She is illegitimate. Her father has a hideout on a rooftop, much like that of Santiago, the little runaway schoolboy. The big tomcat comes down only for food and drink and social affairs, a pattern of living that has merit, in my husband's opinion. And I hid Mona Lisa in a sack, well ventilated, in the trunk of our car before we left the border. My husband didn't hear her meowing until we were well on the way home.

If a social worker can't use her skills to outwit her own husband, why spend all that time and effort acquiring the skills? As Danny would say, everything is rocking along pwutty doggone good.

They Need Not Walk Alone

And so I have told the stories of a few children who were forced, at least for a time, to walk down that lonesome road alone. All of us might well meditate on these factual case histories and speculate on changes for the better.

I could, as a result of my education and career work, speculate for months, going into great detail in discussing changes that might improve the situation. I choose to make only one suggestion: That *all* of us, including school administrators, teachers, and college professors as well as parents, review our attitude toward learning. That we resolve *never* to stop studying and learning. Then, and only then, can we retain an open mind. Only then can we insist on facts instead of prejudicial and often harmful attitudes.

The resistance to learning—to hearing the views of another person or to reading adverse comments about a cherished attitude of our own—seems to harden at certain levels.

I recall the story of a heated exchange between a principal who was having trouble with a veteran case-hardened teacher. "Well, I've had twenty years' teaching experience," she snapped.

"You've had one year of experience and repeated it nineteen times," the principal said.

There is an inevitable tendency on the part of the high school graduate, particularly a deprived youth from a minority ethnic group, to abandon the learning process, assuming that he has all the education he needs. There is an inevitable tendency of the college graduate to assume that there is no further need for study in life. And I am not talking about studying and learning in the formal sense—I mean just keep on learning, keep on analyzing, and keep on growing.

I saw the fallacy of assuming that I had "enough education" after several years in social work. Even though I had a BA and an MA in psychology from an outstanding university, I realized that I was not fully qualified to handle school social work properly. I had been carrying on without an MSW mainly because practically no other school worker had such a degree. But I went to the Graduate School of Social Work of the University of Texas at Austin and spent two years getting a master's in social work. Half that time was spent in field work. I learned from qualified professors and trained supervisors the things a social worker should know. Even after that I have never assumed that my education was complete—that there was no need to learn more. In recent years I have learned much from the graduate students I supervised—they brought a fresh view of the profession.

Learning should continue throughout a person's life, and we have as illustrations the amazing achievements of many persons in their eighties—Verdi, Picasso, Casals, Justice Hugo Black, Churchill, and on and on.

It is true that the person who continues to learn may "walk alone" because he outgrows others. Some teachers do, and the situation can be tragic. Quite often they walk alone because they are still learning—they are filled with enthusiasm and advance new ideas from time to time. They want change—they want to do better things for the children. But . . . they are a lonely minority because too many teachers are like the one who had one year of experience and repeated it nineteen times. For protection, for job security, for serenity, the teacher, like any other person in any walk of life, is likely to settle neatly into the structure and avoid conflict. She "adjusts"—a euphemism for standing still.

It is the easy way out. But all satisfaction in achievement is gone. And what greater reward is there than taking a little child by the hand and leading him away from that lonesome road onto the broad, bright main highway of life?

Lightning Source UK Ltd.
Milton Keynes UK
UKOW04f0335030817
306590UK00001B/94/P